George Grote

Seven Letters concerning the Politics of Switzerland

Pending the Outbreak of the Civil War in 1847

George Grote

Seven Letters concerning the Politics of Switzerland
Pending the Outbreak of the Civil War in 1847

ISBN/EAN: 9783337078874

Printed in Europe, USA, Canada, Australia, Japan

Cover: Foto ©ninafisch / pixelio.de

More available books at **www.hansebooks.com**

SEVEN LETTERS

CONCERNING THE

POLITICS OF SWITZERLAND,

PENDING THE OUTBREAK OF THE CIVIL WAR
IN 1847.

By GEORGE GROTE, Esq.,

AUTHOR OF A "HISTORY OF GREECE."

WITH THE ADDITION OF AN UNPUBLISHED LETTER WRITTEN BY THE
AUTHOR TO M. DE TOCQUEVILLE SHORTLY AFTER
THE TERMINATION OF THE WAR.

LONDON:
JOHN MURRAY, ALBEMARLE STREET.
1876.

LONDON:
PRINTED BY WILLIAM CLOWES AND SONS,
STAMFORD STREET AND CHARING CROSS.

INTRODUCTION.

A REPRINT of the Swiss Letters, originally published in the "Spectator," has been found desirable on more than one ground. For thirty years this passage of domestic strife has only been casually reverted to by attentive observers of political events, and the subject had almost dropped out of the circle of topics possessing a modern interest when the recent German difficulties with the Catholic Church awakened the recollection of the Sonderbund quarrel.

These difficulties have their origin in the very causes which engendered the disturbances of 1847 among the Cantons of Switzerland. On the one hand there is the influence of the Vatican, sustained by the free application of its vast revenues; on the other, an able and resolute representative of the secular power, backed by the authority of a puissant temporal sovereign. It is the same piece playing over again, only that the theatre on which the drama is enacted occupies a more extensive area of territory. The actual dispute excites memories in connection with Swiss affairs, which memories prompt numerous enquiries for the little work of Mr. Grote—a work clearly setting forth the causes of the struggle of 1847, and explaining the complex nature of the political relations existing among the members of that interesting Republic.

But the original edition had long been out of print, and it has not been without difficulty that a copy has been found to meet the demands of those who now desire to re-peruse the "Letters." When it was determined to reprint them, it was deemed a fitting occasion to produce a letter addressed by the Author to M. Alexis de Tocqueville, wherein he takes a retrospective view of the closing incidents of this internecine conflict. It finishes the story, as it were; and the reader will have the leading points more clearly fixed in his mind than they would have been left at the end of Letter VII.

The letter itself was included among a packet

of correspondence restored to the writers, in 1860, by the heirs of M. de Tocqueville.

This contest between the clerical element and the lay element—personfied in the Priest and the Civil Magistrate—is one that will in all probability be maintained, in one quarter of Europe or another, for all time. The actors change, the conditions of the quarrel fluctuate, but the sources of the discord never dry up, and may, in fact, be characterised as sempiternal.

H. G.

LONDON, *March* 1876.

CONTENTS.

LETTER I.

Character of Swiss politics — The Sonderbund — The Diet and its Representatives—M. Guizot's speeches and articles—The Federal Pact—Cantonal selfishness.

LETTER II.

Unpopularity of the Federal Pact—Ultramontanism in the Catholic Cantons — Dr. Strauss' appointment resisted — Disturbances in Zurich — The New Constitution for Lucerne.

LETTER III.

Revision of the Constitutions of Argau and Soleure—Ultramontane tendencies — Politico-religious agitation — The monasteries instigators and promoters of the insurgents— Suppression of four monasteries.

LETTER IV.

Presidential years of the Canton of Lucerne—Contests between the Upper and Lower Valais—The brothers Barman— Young Switzerland—Activity of the Jesuits—Indignation against Lucerne and M. Meyer at the shooting-meeting at Basle—Proposition for the expulsion of the Jesuits brought before the Diet.

Letter V.

The Jesuits introduced into Lucerne—Protest of the Great Council of Zurich—The Corps Francs—Extraordinary Diet at Zurich—Anti-Jesuit feeling—Revolution in the Canton de Vaud.

Letter VI.

Formation of the Sonderbund—Revolution of Berne—Colonel Ochsenbein—Revolution of Geneva—Revision of the Constitution of Bale-Ville—St. Gallen and its population.

Letter VII.

Unitary Government — Lucerne the head of the Catholic *Clerocracy* of Switzerland—The Federal Pact and the Sonderbund—Ameliorated management of the Communes—Education—Pauperism.

Letter to M. de Tocqueville.

Termination of the war in Switzerland—Want of resolution in the Sonderbund—Lord Palmerston's influence in Italy and Switzerland—Dismissal of the Jesuits.

PREFACE.

The following letters embody the results of reading and enquiry during the course of a recent excursion in Switzerland. I thought at first that what I had to say would have been comprised in three letters at farthest; but the matter has insensibly grown under my hands into the bulk of a small volume.

The inhabitants of the twenty-two Cantons of Switzerland are interesting, on every ground, to the general intelligent public of Europe. But to one whose studies lie in the contemplation and interpretation of historical phenomena, they are especially instructive—partly from the many specialities and differences of race, language, religion, civilization, wealth, habits, &c., which distinguish one part of the population from another, comprising between the Rhine and the Alps a miniature of all Europe, and exhibiting the fifteenth century in immediate juxtaposition with the nineteenth—partly from the free and unrepressed action of the people, which brings out such distinctive attributes in full relief and contrast. To myself in particular, they present an additional ground of interest, from a certain political analogy (nowhere else to be found in Europe) with those who prominently occupy my thoughts, and on the history of whom I am still engaged—the ancient Greeks.

In listening not only to the debates in the Diet, but also to the violent expressions of opposite sentiment manifested throughout the country during the present summer, I felt a strong impulse to understand how such dispositions had arisen; to construe the present in its just aspect as a sequel to the past—and to comprehend that past itself in conjunction with the feelings which properly belong to it, not under the influence of feelings belonging to the present. The actual condition, and reasonable promise, of Swiss Federal politics, were different in 1841 and 1844, and have become again materially different in 1847: we have to study each period partly in itself, partly with reference to that which preceded it, and out of which it grew.

A man must have little experience of historical phenomena to suppose that in any violent political contention, all the right is likely to lie on one side and all the wrong on the other. I have not disguised my conviction that both the Swiss parties have committed wrong, nor is my statement likely to give satisfaction to either of them: to shew the prolific power of wrong deeds in generating their like, is in my judgment one of the most important lessons of history. Whether I have distributed praise and blame in right proportion, is a matter on which there is room for difference of opinion; but I shall at least help my readers to conceive the main points of Swiss political dispute in historical sequence, and along with their concomitant circumstances. The English or French criticisms which I have as yet seen, rarely attempt to do this; yet without it no criticism can be either equitable or instructive.

In regard to the future, I am sparing of predictions. Amidst phenomena so complicated, so full of reciprocal excitement, and so little amenable to precedent as those which Switzerland now exhibits, a foreigner can do nothing more than put together the past in order to interpret the present. The business of prediction, as well as that of counsel and guidance, he must leave to natives; and deeply indeed is it to be wished that the Swiss leaders may shew themselves at the actual crisis not incompetent to these lofty functions.

G. G.

LONDON, *October* 14, 1847.

POLITICS OF SWITZERLAND.

Letter I.

Sept. 4, 1847.

Of the numerous travellers who during the course of every summer visit the magnificent scenery of Switzerland, there are not many who interest themselves in the political or social condition of the people. But in the present year, this latter topic has stood to an unusual degree in the foreground; and the proceedings of the Diet, which has been sitting at Berne for the last two months, have attracted more notice than ever that assembly received before, not merely from visitors, but from the general public of Europe. Such increased notice is indeed abundantly justified by the serious character which Swiss politics have now assumed, and by the open collision, seemingly but one degree removed from actual hostilities, of a majority and minority of the Diet. On the

20th of last July, a majority, including twelve Cantons and two Half-Cantons, came to the important vote, that the separate league of seven Cantons, called the Sonderbund, was a contravention of the Federal Pact; directed its dissolution; and threw upon the Cantons composing it the responsibility of all the consequences of disobedience. Those Cantons — Lucerne, Friburg, Schwytz, Unterwalden, Uri, Zug, and Valais — have not only protested against this decision, and refused to obey it, but have even persisted, and are still persisting, in military preparations, for the purpose of repelling any attempt on the part of the majority of the Diet to enforce its decision by arms. As yet, no proposition for forcibly executing the sentence has been submitted to the Diet, whose sentence of condemnation against the Sonderbund has been formally proclaimed, but remains unexecuted. It has been followed up only by one or two other resolutions against the Sonderbund, adopted by the same majority. A supply of arms and ammunition, sent by the Austrians from Lombardy to the Cantons of the Sonderbund, but detained by the inhabitants of Tessin in its passage through that Canton, has been placed under sequestration by order of the Diet, in the hands of the Government of Tessin: the Cantons of the Sonderbund have been formally admonished to discontinue their military preparations: moreover, a Commission has been nominated to examine and communicate with such officers of the Federal military force as hold commissions under the refractory Cantons; and a resolution has been passed by the Diet, to dismiss them from the former unless they voluntarily renounce the latter. Still, no real progress is made towards the dissolution of the Sonderbund; which continues inflexible—obstinate, and even insolent in the language of its Deputies—and unremitting in its warlike preparations. Presently the Diet will also pass a resolution, by the same majority, directing or inviting the expulsion of the Jesuits from Switzerland: but this resolution will meet with the same angry opposition, and the same proclaimed disobedience, as the others.

How long such open dissension can continue, or by what steps it will be brought to a close, no reasonable man will venture to pronounce. But it is most certainly grave and menacing: it is pregnant with the possibility, not to say more, of civil war in Switzerland, and with the further possibility of foreign interference in that country. Assuming even that such interference does not take place, the sympathies of Europe are of no mean account in reference to every individual country; and it is therefore worth while to form some rational estimate of the direction which those sympathies ought to take. The causes of what happens in a Swiss Diet are not a little complicated: for that assembly represents the result of what has been done and felt in each of the twenty-two Cantons—each a little political world, distinct from, though sympathising with, the rest. Switzerland consists of twenty-two Cantons, each having one vote in the Diet, though there is the greatest inequality between them in wealth and population; Berne containing about 430,000 inhabitants, and Zurich about 230,000, while Uri comprises only 15,000. Each Canton is independent and sovereign, except in so far as it is bound by the provisions of the Federal Pact, or by resolutions of the Diet in fulfilment of and in conformity with the Pact. Indeed, even this multiplicity of elements does not represent the full complexity of Swiss political affairs : for three out of the twenty-two Cantons—Bale, Appenzell, and Unterwalden—are divided each into two Half-Cantons, each Half-Canton sovereign and independent, subject to the restriction above mentioned. The two sections of Bale (town and country), and of Appenzell (Inner-Rhoden and Ausser-Rhoden), not only differ from each other on the most material points, but are almost always politically opposed; and whenever they are so opposed, their votes are of course neutralized in the Diet. So multiform are the elements—not to mention the many and important differences of race, religion, language, wealth, civilization, habits, residence in mountain, plain, town, or country, &c.—which go to form political society among the 2,400,000 inhabitants of Switzerland: of whom about 900,000 are Catholics, the remainder Protestants.

To trace the working of these various causes, which have co-operated more or less to form the majority called Radical, and the minority called Conservative, in the present Diet, is no very easy problem even for a native: a foreigner can only seize the principal and prominent circumstances. There is, however, one source of error which especially deserves to be pointed out, and of which more will be said presently—that of estimating the character and tendencies of Swiss parties by the names which they bear of *Radical* and *Conservative*. These names have now got a footing in every language of Europe, and have very strong feelings of esteem or hatred associated with them; they are nowise correct as designations of the two Federal parties prominently opposed in Switzerland, and of the points at issue between them: yet foreigners easily transfer to that country the established sentiments or established interests which they have contracted towards the parties so called at home. This is especially necessary to be borne in mind when we read the speeches delivered by M. Guizot in the French Chamber, or the articles in the *Journal des Débats*, which have so wide a circulation in Europe. Whoever judges of Switzerland from these sources, will carry away an impression not merely partial and inaccurate, but in many respects the direct reverse of real truth.

M. Guizot speaks from the French tribune the language of an exaggerated Swiss party politician: omit the name and translate his speech into German, it might pass for one of the bitter invectives of M. Meyer, the Deputy of Lucerne in the Swiss Diet, against Radical spirit and aggressions. The *Journal des Débats* and other French journals are written in the same vein: to them, as well as to M. Guizot, it is sufficient if they find an opportunity of inflaming their readers against Radical principles, and of impressing upon them the dignity of Conservative politics sanctified by religious zeal. With M. Guizot, probably, such discourses are more than an ebullition of feeling: they are also a useful manœuvre in reference to his own position in France. For he owes that position not to any esteem or confidence entertained towards him by the French people—still less to any hopes which they feel of progress or improvement under his Ministry; but chiefly to the fears which the French electoral body have been taught to entertain of Radicalism. And the menaces, so offensive and indecent in the mouth of any foreign Power, which he addresses to the Swiss Diet, are intended to tell quite as much upon French Conservatives and French Radicals as upon Lucerne and Berne.

Two points deserve particular notice in the bitter animadversions which M. Guizot and the French Conservative journals pour forth against the recent course of Swiss politics.

1. They dwell continually, and almost exclusively, upon two facts in the recent history of that country—the invasion of the Canton of Lucerne, in the end of 1844, as well as in the beginning of 1845, by bands of volunteers from the other Cantons, called the Corps Francs—and the separate league of seven Cantons, called the Sonderbund, which is represented as a consequence of this unjust invasion, and resorted to only as a means of defence.

2. They depict the present majority of twelve Cantons and two Half-Cantons, which has just pronounced the Sonderbund to be unconstitutional and directed its dissolution, as a majority bent upon complete subversion of the Cantonal independent action throughout Switzerland, and upon the transfer of the twenty-two separate Govern-

ments now existing, to one central and united republic at Berne. To add to the terrors of this impending republic, it is described as likely to become aggressive and formidable to all its neighbours; since the 2,400,000 souls which the whole country contains would be so immensely strengthened (we are told) by this concentration, that they would forthwith overstep their own rights and limits, for the purpose and with the power of imposing unjust conditions on others.

Such are the two points principally insisted upon by M. Guizot, and many of the leading critics on Swiss affairs. In regard to the first of the two, they mislead by isolating one single event and presenting it apart from its preceding and accompanying circumstances: in regard to the second, they mislead yet more, by imputing to a great party in Switzerland, designs which none of those who really represent that party have given the least ground for suspecting, and by holding forth as likely to be accomplished a centralization to which all present tendencies stand irrevocably opposed.

That there may be persons in Switzerland, and

those too not among the least patriotic of her citizens, who wish that such a centralization or something approaching to it *could* be established, is probable enough: and it is not easy to see why any impartial foreigner, who desires nothing but the tranquillity, happiness, and improvement of the country, should denounce them for it; although it may suit the purpose of a French Minister, who wishes to see Switzerland at all times open to attack, to foment the maximum of disunion. Among the 2,400,000 people who dwell between the Lakes of Constance and Geneva, there are now twenty-five independent establishments, each fitted up (better or worse) for the complete execution of all the purposes of government. In the time of Aristotle, and with his political experience, such minute subdivision would have appeared an indispensable condition of freedom and responsibility: but in the present state of political knowledge, it is surely neither crime nor folly to conceive that all the great purposes of society might be better fulfilled by locally-chosen governing bodies subordinate to one common centre. And this is the ground actually taken by some of the French Opposition journals against M. Guizot: they seem to admit that the Swiss political leaders do contemplate an entire subordination of the Cantonal to the Central Government, and defend them in this supposed project. Both the attack and the defence are here founded on the same mistaken supposition: still the defence is perfectly well grounded to this extent—that if the Swiss leaders really did entertain the project imputed to them by the French Minister, and were striving to bring their own people to the same view, they would in nowise deserve those bitter denunciations which he has poured forth against them, though the particular circumstances of the case might render it inadmissible and impracticable.

Wise or foolish as the conception of a single or unitary Government, embracing all Switzerland, may be in itself, it is not the conception entertained either by the leading politicians or by any one of the leading Cantons in that country. Revision of the Federal Pact is indeed what they strongly insist upon: but to revise the Pact is one thing — to constitute an unitary or single

Government for the administration of all Switzerland is another. It may safely be pronounced that a revision of the Pact, in such manner as to give too much power to the Central Government and to weaken the Cantonal Governments too much, is of all contingencies the most improbable; though there are so many French and English critics who represent this as a plan already organized by an oppressive majority in Switzerland, and only to be arrested by foreign interference. Of the two extreme and opposite political changes conceivable — first, complete fusion of the Cantonal Governments into one common and unitary Government, or secondly, complete disruption of the Pact and formation of several Governments out of it, altogether distinct from each other—the latter is decidedly the least improbable : nay, if we look at the present unyielding temper and excitement of the Swiss parties it might almost appear the least improbable solution of all, in a problem so essentially embroiled.

The tendencies of the present time, indeed, are not to strengthen the authority of the Diet over the Cantons, but to reduce it still lower—from extreme weakness down to absolute nullity. The conduct of the recusant minority in this present affair of the Sonderbund, and still more the arguments by which they defend that conduct, amount to nothing less than a complete nullification of all imperative authority in the Pact, even as to its most positive and specific provisions. Assuredly, if there is to be any federation at all, one of its most essential provisions must be, that the members shall contract no separate alliances among themselves injurious or dangerous to the entire confederacy. The sixth Article of the Federal Pact distinctly says—" No alliance shall be formed among the several Cantons, detrimental either to the general confederacy or to the rights of other Cantons :" so that, under the terms of this Article, the competence of the Diet to entertain and pronounce upon the legality of the Sonderbund cannot be impugned except by arguments which go to deny its competence universally. Now a majority of the Diet has pronounced the Sonderbund to be illegal and an infringement of the Pact: to which the members of the Sonderbund reply by a protest and a peremptory refusal to obey. Such proclaimed resistance, by so many Cantons at once, is of itself the most fatal blow which has yet been aimed at the authority of the Diet: and the dissolving effect of this practical measure is still further enlarged by the arguments upon which it is made to rest. "We maintain," say the Cantons of this separate league or Sonderbund, "that our league is *not* at variance with the provisions of the Pact; it is purely defensive, and has been rendered necessary by aggressions on the part of other Cantons or their citizens against the Government of Lucerne: we intend no evil to others, if they do not attack us; and we shall maintain our league as long as our own security seems to us to require." To employ such arguments as these while the question was under discussion in the Diet, and for the chance of influencing the decision of that body, was their incontestable right: but they still continue to hold the same language, and act upon the same principle, even after the Diet has decided against them. When it is urged that to apply the general provisions of the Pact to a particular case, and to decide judicially whether the case does or does not fall under a rule there laid down, is among the most indispensable attributes of the Diet—the Sonderbund meet this proposition by an unqualified negative. "We are sovereign Cantons," they say, "and recognise no authority in the majority of the Diet to apply or interpret the Pact against a recusant minority; we admit no right to interpret the Pact except by the unanimous decision of the twenty-two sovereign Cantons; *we* construe the sixth Article of the Pact in a manner perfectly consistent with our separate league, and we shall therefore, as sovereign Cantons, continue to act upon our own construction of it, though a majority of the Cantons may decide otherwise." Here we find an act of avowed and unqualified resistance, sustained by arguments which amount to a complete negation of the authority of the Diet over individual Cantons in any case whatever—to a complete nullification of the Diet as a body acting by its majority. For if the decision of the majority is not to hold good against that of one or a few Cantons, as to the judicial application of an express article of the Pact to a given particular case, it is plainly of no binding authority on any question which may be conceived. The Federal Pact, in this reading, becomes a mere alliance of independent and sovereign States, each of them at liberty to put their own construction upon it and break it whenever they choose—of course at the hazard of war, if contradiction or provocation assume a character sufficiently grave.

Such is the state of public law in Switzerland, as proclaimed and now acted upon by one-third of the twenty-two Cantons, and tacitly sanctioned by a minority, more or less considerable, in the others; and it is strange, in the face of this obvious fact, to hear the French Minister proclaim, that the power to be feared in Switzerland is, an overruling and oppressive interference on the part of the Diet, with an extinction of Cantonal independence! Never before has the judicial competence of the Diet been so glaringly defied in practice, and so explicitly denied in theory, as in the present year; and this too by a very powerful minority. That minority, in the excitement of party contest, may perhaps in part really believe themselves to be the defenders of Cantonal rights unjustly assailed by their opponents; but among them are those who, knowing the case too well to believe in the reality of such danger, also know that the pretence of such belief is the most popular of all topics in reference to Swiss feeling.

It is in fact impossible to study attentively the march of Swiss affairs without seeing, that what really lies next to the hearts of the people is, their Cantonal and communal system; and that, although on some particular questions connected with Swiss Federal politics, there may be rare and temporary moments of excitement—although there is a growing desire, and a very rational desire, for better-assured nationality in the event of foreign danger—nevertheless, the idea of interference on the part of the Diet in Cantonal affairs is habitually unfamiliar and repulsive. This is not less true of the Cantons called Radical than of the Cantons called Conservative — in both of them alike, the citizens look for protection, as well as for command, to their own Cantonal authority. Nothing can be more memorable, throughout the history of the past years, than the uniform indecision and impotence of the Diet; indeed, one reason why so much has been said about terrible projects of over-centralization at the present moment, is, that now, almost for the first time, a majority of the Diet has been found to take a decisive resolution on an important subject. Throughout the past history of the Diet, we find discussion after discussion without determination; no majority at all being found to agree in any—sometimes not even in a negative or vote of rejection. To prevail upon twelve Cantons to agree in any positive vote, has been generally found a difficulty all but insurmountable. Among the many different questions put to the vote, those which are the most trying and important do not often obtain a majority; because several Deputies abstain altogether from voting, some reserving to themselves the liberty of voting, subsequently, when they shall have asked and received instructions from their Canton. It is to be remarked that every Deputy present votes, not agreeably to any opinion of his own, but to instructions received from the Great Council, or supreme legislative authority, in his own Canton—which may sometimes, though this does not often happen, confer upon him plenary powers of self-decision upon some given subject; but, excepting in these cases, the instructions, prepared in each separate Canton, include conditions or adopt modifications different from each other, which usually prevent any number of Deputies from concurring in one substantive proposition. Speaking from his instructions, as a counsel speaks from a brief, a Deputy may sustain his opinion by powerful arguments—and the speeches of some of them are eloquent and creditable; but his conclusion is prescribed to him before the meeting of the Diet. And in fact, the forms and language of the Diet consider each Deputy as an *ambassador* from his Canton: he is always styled " Der Gesandte des Standes——," by the President, when inviting the opinions of every one at the table *seriatim*, and most frequently so styled throughout the course of discussion. The relations of the Deputy to his Canton are doubtless those of a delegate bound by instructions; yet the relations of the Cantons towards each other are not those of independent States, but of States which have bound themselves in confederacy to obey the provisions of a solemn and common Pact, and have formally constituted the body called the Diet to uphold and enforce the Pact.

What the Cantons mostly stand chargeable with is, the feeling of Cantonal selfishness—each being careless of the interests of other Cantons as compared with its own: at least, the tendency to error is almost uniformly in this direction. Thus, when we follow the discussions of the Diet, not upon the present embittered questions of Federal politics, but upon internal taxes, tolls, or commercial regulations in the various Cantons, which fall to a certain extent within its competence—we find this feeling of Cantonal egoism not less prevalent in the Radical Canton of Vaud than in the Sonderbund Cantons of Lucerne and Valais. During the past winter and spring, the suffering from dearth and high prices of provisions being very severe in all parts of Switzerland, each of these three Cantons made regulations either prohibiting or impeding the export of provisions to other Cantons,—a proceeding contrary to the Federal Pact. This subject being brought on for discussion in the Diet shortly after the passing of the vote to dissolve the Sonderbund, the Radical Deputy of Vaud (M. Druey, a coarse but animated and emphatic speaker, not very unlike the late Mr. O'Connell) was found in the same line of defence as the Ultra-Catholic M. de Courten, Deputy of the Valais—the most outspoken and even insolent among all the persons assembled. Whoever imagines that the Radical Cantons are disposed to be liberal in the sacrifice of Cantonal independence to Federal supremacy, would have been undeceived if he had listened to the speech of M. Druey —seasoned, moreover, with many sneers against free trade: he employed one familiar comparison which illustrates the relation of the Cantonal to the Federal feelings throughout Switzerland— "My shirt is nearer to me than my coat." In the course of another discussion, in which the Conservative Canton of Valais was proved to be upholding a scheme of tolls not only at variance with the Pact, but also without that formal communication, in respect to tolls imposed, which every Canton is bound to furnish to the Federal authority, the

Deputy of Valais, M. de Courten, went so far as to tell the Diet flatly—"Nous n'y renoncerons jamais." So jealous and irritable is the sentiment of Cantonal independence on both sides, even in matters where the rights of conscience are noway concerned, and where the matter in dispute is nothing greater than the raising of revenue in one way rather than in another. To show the different cross-divisions among the Cantons, I may add, that Neufchatel, which is highly Conservative in general politics, and makes almost common cause with the Sonderbund, though not a member of it, is at the same time extremely liberal and right-minded on questions of trade and transit.

If we except the arrangements for the Federal military force,—for the relations between Switzerland and foreign countries, and for some few questions of toll and transit—on all other points the Cantonal Governments may be said to act without any positive interference on the part of the Diet. Doubtless the Pact, with its solemn recognition of a common country and brotherly obligation between the Cantons, exercises a considerable moral influence over their proceedings; and the meetings of the Diet, in spite of the feebleness of its coercive sanction, are indispensably necessary to keep alive and strengthen this moral influence. Hence arises a partial disposition, feebler than might be desired, yet still precious, to adapt their legislation to the interests of each other—and a facility for special agreements between them having this object in view. Yet that the Pact itself ought also to be modified, so as to enlarge the attributions of the Diet and impart to the country a more efficient and better protected nationality, has long been a widespread conviction in Switzerland, and seems as a general position not denied even by the Government of Lucerne; though that Canton, as well as the other Cantons of the Sonderbund, protests against attempting to alter it at the present time and under present feelings. And the Diet itself has on several occasions entertained the general idea of revising the Pact, though no specific plan has ever found approval: it has again in its present session, by the same majority which pronounced the Sonderbund to be illegal, decided that the Pact required alteration, and that a Committee should be appointed to make a report on the best means of attaining this end. It is remarkable, that every one of the Deputies who formed this majority, disclaimed in the most emphatic manner the idea imputed to them, of surrendering Cantonal independence and aiming at an unitary Government in Switzerland. This Committee, composed of all the Deputies of the majority—it could hardly be otherwise composed, since the Deputies of the Sonderbund refused to take part in the proceeding—are now assembled; and it will remain to be seen whether they can agree in recommending any positive scheme of real importance and efficiency. One effect can hardly fail to ensue from their report—a complete refutation of that charge of anti-Cantonal tendency which is so loudly urged against them by the Sonderbund and its foreign partisans. But whether these Deputies will all be able to concur in any specific plan of reform, with due respect to this limit—still more, whether their respective Cantons (in each of which there is a Conservative minority ready to raise opposition on any plausible ground, and in many of which there are Catholics more or less open to the intrigues of Lucerne) will all concur in adopting their recommendation—must remain for the future to decide: should matter proceed even so far as this, there will still remain the Sonderbund, a large minority who will oppose anything and everything. Yet, assuming such unqualified repugnance on the part of the Sonderbund for the present to continue, still, if the existing majority of Cantons, comprising four-fifths of the population, and more than four-fifths of the intelligence and wealth of Switzerland, should agree in sanctioning any definite reform of the Federal Pact—above all, if a sentiment should grow up among them of deeper attachment and more willing submission to the Pact so improved, than that which is felt towards the Pact as it now stands—a great point will be gained for the future march, organization, and tranquillity of Switzerland. Berne and Zurich, the first and second among the Cantons in respect of population and power, are on this occasion in cordial co-operation, —a rare conjunction, since jealousy between these two powerful Cantons is among the standing phenomena of Swiss politics. And this increases materially the chance both of arriving at some definite result in respect to Federal reform, and of repressing disorderly ebullitions amidst the conflicting elements with which Switzerland is now disturbed.

In touching upon Swiss affairs, the first impulse of an impartial observer is to repel those false charges which M. Guizot—with a looseness of speech altogether unbecoming in a statesman of his position—has advanced against the majority of the Diet. I shall in a future letter say something respecting that series of preliminary events, one growing out of another, which has brought about the present serious conflict of parties in Switzerland. Though it cannot for a moment be contended that all the right is on one side and all the wrong on the other, yet, if we look for the great cause both of mischief in the past and of danger for the future, we shall find it in the statesmen, miscalled Conservative, who are now at the head of the Government of Lucerne.

LETTER II.

Sept. 11, 1847.

THE Federal Pact under which the Swiss Cantons now live has become unpopular not merely from its own intrinsic defects and ambiguities, but also from the time and circumstances of its origin. It was framed in 1815, in place of the constitution called the Act of Mediation; which, having been introduced and guaranteed by Napoleon, had fallen with the extinction of his power. It was the product of a time when the patrician families in politics and Ultramontane influences in religion were in a state of triumphant reaction against the restraints imposed upon them from 1798 downward: both of them seconded by the Allied Powers at the Congress of Vienna; who, however, to their credit be it spoken, mitigated on several points the exorbitant pretensions of the revived native oligarchies. Since 1830, almost all the Cantonal Governments have undergone a capital change, and have become thoroughly popular: so that the Federal Pact remains as the only unaltered relic of an odious time. In 1832, the majority of the Diet recognised the necessity of modifying it, and named a Committee for the purpose, of which M. Rossi of Geneva was the reporter. Their scheme of Federal reform—maintaining intact the Cantonal sovereignty and equal representation in the Diet, but remodelling the Federal authority, and introducing in every way valuable improvements—was signed by the Deputies of fourteen Cantons (including the three directing Cantons of Berne, Zurich, and Lucerne), and recommended by them earnestly to the acceptance of Switzerland. Unhappily for the country, it was rejected; chiefly from the resolute opposition of the primitive and Conservative Cantons, who would endure no change at all—partly from the indifference, rather than the opposition, of extreme politicians on the other side, who wished for something more comprehensive and symmetrical.

Prior to the year 1798, the condition of a Swiss Canton was that of a great feudal lord, with an aggregate of many separate seigneurial properties, acquired partly by conquest, partly by purchase: in the town Cantons—such as Berne, Soleure, Basle, Zurich, &c.—the town was the lord, the country districts were attached to it as dependent properties: in the rural Cantons—such as Uri, Schwytz, &c.—it was an aggregate of rural and democratical communes which exercised lordship over other dependent communes in their neighbourhood. This system of profound political inequality, broken up between 1798 and 1815, was revived to a great degree in the latter year: in the town Cantons, the Government again fell into the hands of the citizens of the town, and was even confined to a small number of persons among those citizens; while the country districts were either essentially subject, or had a share in it little more than nominal. Most of the Cantons had their two Councils—Great and Small Council; the former legislative, the latter executive: but the real powers of government were all exercised by the Small or Executive Council, while the Great Council had neither initiative, nor independent play of its own, nor publicity of debate; but was in practice a mere acquiescent adjunct of the

Executive, rather than a check upon it. In the Catholic Cantons, the reaction of 1815 took the form of a devoted Ultramontanism; the governing few surrendering themselves to the inspirations of the Papal Nuncio with a compliance not paralleled in any part of Europe, and forming a strong contrast with the resolute independence of the old Catholic Cantons before 1798 in maintaining their civil authority against the Court of Rome. In the Canton of Valais, this Ultramontanism reached its maximum; the priests being subject to a special jurisdiction for their persons, and enjoying immunity from taxation as to their properties, in a manner more suitable to the fifteenth century than to the nineteenth. The primitive Cantons of Uri, Unterwalden, and Schwytz (the latter with modifications in consequence of the unequal relation of what were called the outer districts), retained their old primitive constitution unchanged: the Landesgemeinde, or general assembly of all the adult citizens, meets once in the year, has the exclusive power of making laws when needed, and elects the administrators required, who are very seldom changed. Such form of Democracy is universally acceptable to the people of these Cantons: though, when taken in conjunction with their dull and stationary intelligence, their bigotry, and their pride in bygone power and exploits, it works in practice as a mere routine of power, practically secret and irresponsible, in the hands of a small number of old families; very different from the Canton of Appenzell Ausser Rhoden, where substantially the same form of government prevails among a population industrious, orderly, intelligent, and public-spirited, far beyond the average of Switzerland.

These Swiss Governments, all springing out of the reaction of 1815, acted in harmony with each other as to general politics; though even then, in questions of fiscal and internal administration, the spirit of Cantonal egoism was not less rife than it is at present. Moreover, they were all, in the proper sense of the word, *Conservative* Governments—founded upon privilege and exclusion of the mass of the people from political power—satisfied to remain stationary in this system, doing nothing in the way of correction or amelioration, and leaving the separate communes in the Cantons to their own management or mismanagement; but prudent in respect to their finances, and true to the old Swiss idea of keeping a public fund in hand bearing interest. During the last years before 1830, however, a public feeling was gradually growing up against these oligarchies; so that even before the French Revolution of July, the people of some Cantons had begun to demand, and that of Tessin had actually obtained, a measure of popular reform. But the Revolution of July roused the public mind throughout nearly all Switzerland: during the few years following, the Governments of Berne, Zurich, Argau, Soleure, Lucerne, Friburg, Schaffhausen, Thurgau, St. Gallen, and Glarus, became all popularized; the changes being carried without bloodshed, but by the same sort of intimidation which, in 1832, pushed the English Reform Bill through the House of Lords—meetings and demonstrations of sentiment such as the actual Governments were unable to resist. These movements—directed to obtain recognition of the sovereignty of the people, with an elective franchise exercised by the people alike in town and country—were properly Radical movements, just as the party in power to which they were opposed was Conservative; it was then that the denominations *Radical* and *Conservative* became current in reference to the two opposing parties; and they have continued to be so applied after their fitness and appropriate meaning had to a great degree ceased.

During the years immediately after 1830, the Governments of most of the Cantons became thus thoroughly popularized. The privilege of town over country which had been the characteristic mark of the previous oligarchies, was first diminished and has been subsequently effaced; for though in the first changes an artificial preponderance was still left to the town in the number of its representatives compared with those of the country, such preponderance has since been annulled, and the suffrage has become practically equal and universal. Moreover, the Great or Legislative Council was exalted to be the controlling superior of the Executive; it debated publicly, under the stimulus of an active press, with meetings, and all the exaggerated movement of a vigorous political life. The preceding Conservative functionaries were replaced by men of the movement and either retired from public life or were thrown into opposition. To regain power as avowed Conservatives, or champions of the old privileges, was impracticable; they were obliged to accept and work under the popular forms, by appealing to some feeling in the public mind; and it was in this manner that religion came to be invoked as a weapon of excitement for political purposes.

The first memorable manifestation of this new phase of Swiss political life took place on the 6th of September, 1839, at Zurich; where the Radical Government was violently overthrown, in consequence of their nomination of Dr. Strauss to a chair of theology. Not only did the political opposition in the Council, the public, and the press, raise the most vehement outcry against this appointment, but the clergy (most of whom had received their appointments from, and sympathized with, the prior Government before 1830) employed their pulpits in the most direct and exciting manner against the Government; which was obliged to give way, and cancel the nomination. Had the matter stopped here, no one (whether assenting with their opinions or not) would have had any right to blame them. But having gained this point, they found the path too promising not to push on farther. They organised what were called Committees of Faith, composed of clergymen as well as laymen; preached insurrection throughout the villages adjoining Zurich; prevailed upon a large number of the rural population to take up arms under the cry of "Religion in danger," and marched into the town to put down the Government by force. A clergyman named Hirzel was actually at the head of these armed assailants; who overpowered the resistance opposed to them, and drove the Executive Council out of the city. One of the members of that Council, Dr. Hegetschwyler, in endeavouring to restore peace, was among those slain in the streets. This violent revolution—in consequence of which the Government of Zurich passed entirely into the hands of the politico-religious party (still called Conservative) who had made it—took place at the time when not only Zurich was presiding Canton of the Confederation, but when the Diet was actually assembled in the town.

If the religious feelings of the population admitted of being turned so profitably to party account in a Protestant Canton like Zurich, much more could they be so employed by Catholic leaders and priests amidst a Catholic population. And this was the movement which really took place in those Catholic Cantons which had been liberalized after 1830. In Lucerne and Soleure—and even in Friburg, though to a less decided extent—new and popular constitutions had been promulgated in 1831, and the Government had come into the hands of the leading Liberal politicians in the Cantons. The old Conservative party and the Ultramontane priests joined to form an opposition against them : and though the Lucerne Government had given no such plausible ground to that opposition as the nomination of Dr. Strauss furnished at Zurich, nevertheless the ascendency of the Catholic hierarchy and clergy was sufficiently cramped by the constitution of 1831 to induce them to raise the cry of danger to religion. The year 1840 was the year predetermined for submitting the constitutions of Lucerne, Soleure, and Argau, to decennial revision. In the elections which took place in the first half of that year throughout the Canton of Lucerne, for choosing a constituent body empowered to review and propose amendments in the constitution of 1831, the party called Conservative, with the Ultramontane clergy, were completely successful, and a majority of the constituent body were chosen in a sense hostile both to the existing constitution and to the existing Government. This change was effected in a manner constitutional and pacific, very different from the revolution at Zurich in the preceding year; but it was effected under a similar rallying cry, and gave a triumph to reactionary influences in both Cantons, which were at first in hearty sympathy with each other.

The new constitution framed by these so-called Conservatives, and accepted by the people of Lucerne in 1841, was, however, no return to Conservatism as it had stood between 1815 and 1830. On the contrary, it was a great deal more Radical (measuring Radicalism by the extent of direct power given to the people) than that which the Radicals themselves had framed in 1831. The grand object was to enlarge the power of the

Catholic ecclesiastics, and to render them as completely independent of lay authority as the people could be persuaded to tolerate. The constitution of 1831 had been a representative Democracy: that of 1841 (called by some Swiss writers a Theocratic Ochlocracy) introduced, among other changes, the popular veto, or power of submitting to the vote of the people throughout the Canton, all laws passed by the Legislative Council. On the supposition that this Council should pass any law unacceptable to the priests, the priests had thus a good chance of procuring its rejection by the people. By enfeebling the lay ascendency, more room was made for the ecclesiastical. To illustrate the interest of the Catholic ecclesiastics in this arrangement, we may mention, that in the Canton of Valais, where their power is greater than in any other part of Europe, and where (as has already been observed) they even enjoy complete immunity from taxation for their large property, as well as a special jurisdiction for their persons—in the Valais there subsists not merely the popular veto, but even what is called the *referendum*; that is, every law passed by the Representative Council not only *may*, if required, be submitted to the vote of the primary assemblies, but it *must* in every case be so submitted, before it acquires validity.

In the Canton of Zurich, the party which acquired power by the revolution of 1839, lost it in 1845 by the quiet change of electoral majority—partly from causes which will presently be explained, but partly also from the shame now felt for the means whereby that revolution was accomplished. In the Canton of Lucerne, the case is otherwise: the party who acquired power in 1841 have retained it ever since; and to them, more than to any other cause whatever, the subsequent bitter dissensions of Switzerland, as well as the present almost inextricable embarrassments in the way of future union, are to be traced. They are animated with an indefatigable Ultramontane zeal, and have constituted themselves the central point of Catholic Switzerland, for the protection and extension of the political interests of that church. Of the way in which this disposition has been manifested more will be said in a future letter: but it is impossible to comprehend the present condition of Swiss politics unless we go back to that alliance of clerical aggressiveness and ambition with the employment of religion as a party engine, by Conservative or Anti-Radical politicians, which first manifested itself in Zurich and Lucerne in 1839 and 1840.

LETTER III.
Sept. 18, 1847.

IT has already been stated, in the preceding letter, that the Cantons of Soleure and Argau were destined to a revision of their political constitutions (both established in 1831) during the course of 1840, in like manner with Lucerne. Soleure is entirely Catholic: Argau is a Canton of parity, divided between Protestants and Catholics in the proportion of about three-fifths to two-fifths, but recognising equality of political rights between the two confessions. In both these Cantons Ultramontane tendencies, the same as in Lucerne, had been active since 1831: "Catholic unions," formed throughout most of the villages in these Cantons, as well as in the Catholic portion of Berne, were worked through public meetings and the press, as well as by the pulpit and the confessional, to inculcate the religious duty incumbent on Catholics of liberating the hierarchy from civil control, and aggrandizing them at the expense of the civil power; and so impatient did this feeling become, that the Catholics near Porentru in Berne, as well as those in the neighbourhood of the convent of Muri in Argau, actually rose in armed insurrection against their Governments in the course of 1835. Both movements were put down by military force, and in both cases the parties concerned were treated with remarkable mildness. Proceedings by violence were thus repressed; but the Ultramontane agitation still continued, and reached its height during the year 1840, appointed for revision. On that occasion, the party might well hope to obtain their purpose by pacific means; and as they had been completely successful in the elections in Lucerne during the first half of that year, so they were encouraged to anticipate the same result in Soleure and Argau during the last half. At that time there were eight monasteries in the Canton of Argau—four of nuns and four of monks; two of the latter, Muri and Wettengen, both rich. These convents were, throughout 1840, the great seats of the politico-religious agitation then going forward. While the leaders from the three Cantons held meetings and concerted their measures there, the ample funds of the convents were not spared for the movement; which was impressed upon the neighbouring population as a religious cause in the strictest sense, and enforced as well by the strongest appeals which the Catholic faith and the authority of priests and monks could furnish, as by unmeasured cries of irreligion against opponents.

Notwithstanding these strenuous efforts, however, the movement was not successful either in Soleure or in Argau. In both of them, the revising assemblies proposed projects of amended constitutions, containing neither that extension of Catholic privilege as compared with Protestant, and Catholic church-power as compared with lay-power —nor that introduction of direct appeal to the people in veto or *referendum*—which the leaders in this triple Cantonal agitation demanded: their projects were submitted to the votes of the general body of citizens, and sanctioned by large majorities. Respecting the Canton of Argau, two circumstances deserve notice—First, that the constitution of 1831 (then under revision) not only placed the Catholics under no political disadvantages as compared with the Protestants, but even gave them more than reasonable privileges; for in spite of their inferior numbers, and their still greater inferiority in wealth, industry, and intelligence, it secured to them a numerical half of the members of the Great Council. Secondly, although there were thus no real political grievances of Catholics to be removed, nevertheless the revising Council was at first so influenced by the powerful agitation going forward, that they proposed a scheme of constitution in which a portion of the Catholic claims were conceded; and this scheme, on being submitted to vote, was rejected, not merely by Protestants, who thought the concessions unreasonable, but also by the Catholics themselves, who despised them as insufficient, and thought that a second trial with persevering efforts would extort more. But they were disappointed: the attempt at conciliation having failed, the second scheme which was proposed made no unreasonable concessions to Catholic demands—proceeded upon reason and justice—and was accepted by a large majority of the citizens on the 5th January, 1841. Even this constitution, however (the one still subsisting), though it did not grant the Catholic demands, is still politically such as to favour Catholics at the expense of Protestants. For the Argovian Executive Council consists of nine members, of whom four must be Catholics and four Protestants; the ninth may belong to either confession. The Supreme Judicial College is divided in the same manner. Considering the inferiority of the Catholics in number (not to mention other points of inferiority), the constitution, even as it now stands, thus gives them justice and something more. It is right to add that these revisions were, on almost all points, material improvements on the constitutions as they had stood before, both in Argau and Soleure.

These two votes, both in Soleure and Argau, took place nearly at the same time; and the disappointment as well as exasperation of those who guided the systematic agitation which pervaded both Lucerne and these two Cantons was extreme. Not choosing to acquiesce in the pacific solution which had gone against them, they had recourse to arms: simultaneous risings took place both in Soleure and Argau, with the instigation and concurrence of the brother agitators in Lucerne. In

Argau, that rising took place among the Catholic population of the Southern districts, or Freien Aemter, near to the borders of Lucerne: it was in the immediate neighbourhood of the convents, whose inmates fomented it in every way—their buildings having been made places for the concealment of arms and munitions, their funds employed to distribute money, wine, and brandy, among the insurgents—and their armed servants and dependents in the foremost ranks of the latter. The purpose of the insurgents was to march directly upon Aarau, the chief town of the Canton, to overpower the Government, and to erect their own portion of Argau into a separate Canton apart from the rest—a little Catholic neighbour and appendage of Lucerne. They also did what they could to provoke a simultaneous rising among the Catholics of the Frickthal (on the northern side of the Canton of Argau, near the left bank of the Rhine, wherein are Laufenburg and Rheinfelden). But these latter Catholics remained quiet, and refused to take any part: they were not in the neighbourhood or under the direct influence of the convents.

It happened that both the Government of Soleure and that of Argau were strong enough to suppress these dangerous risings: the latter, however, only by the aid of troops from Berne. The Catholic insurgents in the Freien Aemter were put down and disarmed: the insurgent leaders both from Soleure and Argau, as well as the monks out of the implicated convents, fled to Lucerne for refuge: some of the parties seized were tried before the ordinary courts of justice, but neither as to person nor property was any extraordinary severity displayed towards them. As a consequence of this insurrection the Argovian Great Council was forthwith assembled, and one of its first measures was to decree the suppression of the convents. Provision for life was made for the existing inmates: subject to this deduction, all the remaining conventual properties were consecrated to the religious worship, the instruction, the charitable purposes, and general welfare of the Catholic communes in the district around—those very communes most of which had just been engaged in actual insurrection.

That this suppression of convents sprang neither

from rapacity nor from any feeling hostile to Catholic citizens or the Catholic faith, is sufficiently shown by the act of appropriation last mentioned—the application made of the property : moreover, the decree was proposed in Council by one of the leading Catholics in Argau—Augustin Keller, Director of the Catholic Seminary—and received the support of many Catholic members. There is, however, in the Federal Pact an Article expressly relating to the convents, guaranteeing their perpetuity as they were found in 1815, so far as the Cantons in which they stand are concerned: this twelfth Article is historically known to have been inserted at the urgent instance of the Papal Nuncio, contrary to the wish of most of the Cantons even in their then reactionary spirit. When the Diet assembled shortly after this transaction, the Canton of Lucerne preferred loud complaints against the suppression of the Argovian convents, as a robbery, an outrage on the Catholic faith, and a direct violation of the twelfth Article in the Pact; the plenary application of which Lucerne invoked at the hands of the Diet—total, unconditional, and compulsory restitution of all the convents and their property. The Deputy of Argau defended the act of his Canton by alleging the flagrant rebellion of which the convents had recently been accomplices and instigators: such appeal to arms on their part had forfeited their title to the Federal guarantee, and rendered their continuance inconsistent with the security and authority of the Cantonal Government. Though the sentiment of the majority of the Diet was unfavourable to the recent proceeding of the Canton of Argau, they nevertheless did not go so far as to accede to the proposition of Lucerne: the majority passed a resolution disapproving generally what had been done by Argau, and requiring that it should be modified, but without expressly prescribing how. The Argovian Government was constrained to conform to this sentiment, and offered to restore three out of the four suppressed female convents: this compromise, however, was not deemed sufficient to satisfy an entire majority of the Diet, and the question remained under long and angry debate during the sittings both of 1841 and 1842—no majority being obtained for any positive conclusion. At length, in the session of 1843, the Canton of Argau enlarged its offer of compromise by proposing to restore all the four suppressed female convents. So enlarged, the offer was held to be satisfactory by the majority of the Diet, and a vote was passed in the session of 1843 to treat the subject as settled : not without the strongest protest, however, from a considerable minority, including Lucerne.

The question of the Argovian convents was thus closed, as far as the majority of the Diet could close it; but it has been revived in discussion over and over again; and even during the present year M. Bernard Meyer, the Deputy of Lucerne, pronounced it to have been the beginning of all the present evils of Switzerland. He chose to call it a *beginning*, and to forget the circumstances which had preceded : and your correspondent, " A Genevese," in inquiring why the Diet did not interfere to protect the property of the Argovian convents, appears to treat the suppression as if it were a simple question between a robber on one side and a party robbed on the other; though in reality there is no incident with respect to which it is more essential to observe his own admonition, " not to state an affair as a mere question of law without reference to antecedent circumstances." If ever there was a proceeding which grew out of, and was imperiously driven on by, antecedent circumstances, it was the suppression of the convents of Argau. In my judgment the Diet interfered in enforcement of the Pact quite as far as the case justified them, not to say farther: they procured the restitution of four convents out of the eight; and if the "Genevese" thinks that they ought to have taken up and executed the demand of Lucerne for total and unconditional restitution, I dissent from his view. To compel the restitution of the convent of Muri—probably the instigator of the insurrection among the Catholics around it in 1835, and certainly the foremost among the rebellious convents in 1841—would have been a blow not merely to Cantonal Government, but also to all civil Government as compared with ecclesiastical immunity, more worthy of the time of Gregory the Seventh than of the nineteenth century. In the Catholic kingdoms of Bavaria and Austria, how many days' purchase would the existence of a convent be worth if its monks were strongly suspected of having raised a first insurrection, and certainly known to have raised a second? Estimate Cantonal rights as low as you will, no reasonable man will believe that the Cantons who signed the Pact of 1815 intended to guarantee the inviolability of convents caught in flagrant rebellion.

As we descend from 1843 down to the present time, we shall find that one party-wrong begets another; and if we are to look for what M. Meyer calls the *beginning*, we must go back farther than the suppression of the Argovian convents. Such suppression, under the particular circumstances of the case, may well be contended to have been no wrong at all, but a step justified by the past, and essential as a protection and remedy for the future: if we even admit that it was a wrong, we must at the same time admit that it grew out of a previous wrong—the rebellion of the convents. That rebellion, connected both in time and in origin with the rising against the Government of Soleure, was the last resort of a widespread political religious agitation, and of a string of active "Catholic unions" which pervaded the Cantons of Lucerne, Argau, Soleure, and Catholic Berne, during the years immediately preceding 1841. These Catholic unions had of course the fullest right to enforce their views by public discussion and appeal. Nay, let us even grant, large as the concession is, that they had a right to resort as they did to an unscrupulous employment of religious hopes and fears, to promise the blessing of the saints and to denounce opponents as heretics beyond the pale of salvation, for the purpose of procuring such changes as they desired in the political constitution—still the votes of the whole people were collected on the subject of this constitution, the decision was against them, and there their rights ended. To take arms against that decision was a political wrong, not only clear and decisive, but unprovoked, unbegotten by any previous wrong. It was the cry of "Religion in danger," employed to put arms into the hands of Catholic insurgents, just as the same cry, sixteen months before, had been successfully used by Protestants to overthrow by force the Government of Zurich: and the Capuchin friar who, in January

1841, headed the Argovian Catholic insurgents on their march against Aarau, forms a parallel to the Protestant clergyman M. Hirzel who, on the 6th September, 1839, conducted the armed zealots of the country round Zurich into that city. The same phænomenon appears in both—the intrusion of direct and violent religious agency in politics; by the Conservative Protestants, as an antithesis and diversion to political Radicalism; by the Catholic leaders, as a nominal reinforcement of popular control, but a real transfer of power from the laity to the priesthood. This phænomenon manifests itself largely throughout the Swiss world towards the period which we are now examining; and it requires to be understood if we would follow the train of events down to the Jesuits and the Sonderbund. For a certain time, these two movements are in sympathy with one another: leaders at Zurich opposed to Radicalism in their own Canton, were not displeased to see it exaggerated in name, but degraded into a secondary force and becoming a mere implement of the altar, although by a Catholic hierarchy, in the Catholic Cantons; and, in 1841, the Government of Zurich, then presiding Canton, friendly to Lucerne and hostile to Argau, was even displeased with Berne for having furnished those troops to the Argovian Government, which enabled it promptly to put down the insurrection. This sympathy between the Government, called Conservative, at Zurich, which acquired power by the insurrection of the 6th September, 1839—and the Ultramontane Government of Lucerne, since 1840—proved after a certain time the cause of the overthrow of the former; the subsequent conduct of Lucerne, as will be hereafter mentioned, having been such as to alienate the population of the Canton of Zurich.

As to the question of Federal right involved in the suppression of the convents, the majority of the Diet must be held to be the only competent judges,—unless, indeed, we are to admit the doctrine now laid down by the Sonderbund, that every Canton has a right to interpret the Pact for itself; in which case the Canton of Argau would of course be as much in the right as its opponents. According to the verdict of that majority, the suppression of the convents of monks must be held to have been justified by sufficient reasons;

that of the other four not justified. The Government of Argau, having at first partially done wrong, made expiation, and put itself right with the Diet. This is a matter to be recollected when we come to discuss the recent conduct of the Sonderbund.

But, apart from the question of right, how far were the Catholics of Argau gainers or losers by the suppression? Whoever reads one of the most interesting books published in modern times—the Autobiography of the historian Zschokke, of Aarau—will find an authentic account of three out of the eight monasteries as they stood in 1833, seven years before the suppression; especially of the convent of Muri. M. Zschokke, together with two Catholic gentlemen, was named Inspecting Visitor of the Monasteries by the Argovian Government. He found the population around the convent of Muri the idlest, poorest, most barbarous, and most ignorant, in the whole Canton: a long train of able-bodied beggars of both sexes to be seen at the doors of the monastery, dirty and in rags, receiving distributions of soup from the kitchen—but exhibiting the lowest average both of physical and moral well-being throughout the neighbouring villages. Unquestionably, the Catholic population around the monastery has been the real gainer by its suppression: the Cantonal Government has acquired nothing in a pecuniary point of view, but it has gained unspeakably in respect of assured position, by being relieved from a rich establishment always ready to pay for an insurrection among the neighbouring Catholics, on the strength of its assured Federal inviolability, whenever the priestly party in Lucerne might be disposed to give the word. The present sentiment of these Catholic parts of Argau has now become much more favourable towards their own Cantonal Government; and it deserves to be mentioned that they, as immediate neighbours of Lucerne, were the great sufferers by the severe measures which the Lucerne Government adopted last winter to restrict the exportation of provisions: they were obliged to throw themselves on their own Government, which made unavailing applications to Lucerne for relaxation. This transaction has tended not only to alienate their feelings from Lucerne, but also to throw them into connexion with the markets of Zurich; a tendency which will probably be farther facilitated by the railway recently opened from Zurich to Baden, the central point of Catholic Argau.

The compromise respecting the Argovian convents was carried into effect in the spring of 1843: an explanation of that event with its preliminary circumstances has been unavoidably necessary, partly because it produced a great effect on Federal proceedings, partly because it ushered in the state of things in 1843, which will be touched upon in the next letter. The Presidency of Lucerne occupies the years 1843 and 1844; and the Presidential conduct of that Canton (especially in regard to the revolution of Valais, to be hereafter noticed), constitutes the immediate preliminary to the Jesuits, the Corps Francs, and the Sonderbund.

LETTER IV.

Sept. 25, 1847.

THE years 1843 and 1844, as has been mentioned in the last letter, were the presidential years of the Canton of Lucerne. Such exercise of the Federal executive authority, not by any special magistrate or council, but by the Council of one or other of the three directing Cantons, has of course the inconvenience, among many others, of causing the employment of Federal authority to be more or less guided by the politics actually prevalent in each of the three. In the project of reform drawn up by M. Rossi and the Commission of 1833, this inconvenience was pointed out, and a special Federal Executive, apart from all the Cantonal Governments but under the control of the Diet, was proposed to be created. More or less partiality in the management of the directing Canton is certain, and has been witnessed in Berne and Zurich as well as in Lucerne. But in the conduct of the latter during 1844, such partiality exceeded all pardonable limits, and all former parallel: it degenerated into grave and manifest treason, and contributed essentially to rouse against that Canton the strong animosity which we shall find breaking out in December 1844 and April 1845.

Though Lucerne in these last months of 1844 was thrown upon the defensive, and suffered from the wrongful assaults of others, the case was otherwise during the time which preceded: that Canton was then the forward and aggressive mover. I have already noticed the politico-religious agitation throughout the Catholic unions in Lucerne, Soleure, and Argau, and Catholic Berne, down to 1841: the defeat of the insurrections in Soleure and Argau disappointed without extinguishing the Ultramontane spirit. Shortly after Lucerne came to the presidency, the Government of Argau found itself exposed to farther agitation, and to fresh attempts at insurrection; which, however, it was strong enough to put down. Lucerne became associated with the League of Sarnen, to which it had stood decidedly opposed previous to 1840. That league was formed about 1832, for the purpose of resisting the Liberal or Radical tendencies then current throughout Switzerland: it consisted originally of Uri, Schwytz, and Underwalden, to which subsequently Friburg, Zug, and Lucerne, and lastly (after the counter-revolution of 1844) the Valais, became added: it is in fact an earlier stage of the present Sonderbund, only that the Sonderbund has been drawn tighter and provided with a formal military organisation. In the year 1843, the plan entertained, and much talked of by the State Gazette of Catholic Switzerland (a journal then published at Lucerne), was to form a great separate league comprehending all the Catholic Cantons, for the protection of the Catholic religion against the oppression and peril under which it was alleged to labour: Soleure was to be either gained over or counter-revolutionized. M. Munzinger, the Deputy of Soleure, read in the Diet during discussions of the present year 1847, the plan of this great Catholic Sonderbund, which Lucerne had circulated in his Canton during the year 1843, but which found little favour among the Solothurnian citizens: moreover, the same scheme of a separate league was so distinctly announced in the resolution of the Great Council of

Lucerne of 20th October, 1843, that both Berne and Zurich protested against it as tending to the breaking up of the Confederacy, and forwarded their protest in circular to all the Cantons. In point of fact the Catholic religion neither had then, nor has now, any oppression to complain of in Switzerland: if there were ground for complaint on the side of either of the two confessions, it would be with the Protestants, who are excluded from all political rights in Lucerne and its confederate Cantons, while there is no analogous exclusion of Catholics in the Cantons mostly Protestant.

It was during the year 1843 that the political state of the Canton of Valais became disordered, and that the foundation was laid for Federal interference in its affairs. That Canton is altogether Catholic: but the two portions of which it consists—the Upper and Lower Valaisans—are of different race and language; and down to 1798 the latter, although more numerous, having been originally conquered by the former, remained their subjects. Suspended or abated between 1798 and 1815, the privileges of the Upper Valaisans were partially revived in 1815, when an imperfect representative constitution was established, with unjust preponderance to the Upper Valais, and with a large fraction of the representation vested in the Bishop of Sion. For several years after 1830, the Lower Valaisans attempted to obtain a political reform, which was at length finally accomplished in April 1840, after opposition both of fraud and force on the part of the Upper Valaisans aided by their clergy, and after much indirect discouragement thrown in their way by the Conservative Government of Zurich, then directing the Canton of Vorort.

The fate of the Liberal Government in the Valais, at the head of which were the two brothers Maurice and Joseph Barman, during its short-lived career from April 1840 to May 1844, forms one of the most melancholy pages of recent history. Its leaders were among the most patriotic and most instructed men in the Canton: they went straight to practical, genuine, and serious reforms, but with strict respect for legal means, and with as little offence as possible towards the prejudices opposed to them: they stand chargeable with various faults of weakness and misjudgment, but the greatest of all their errors was that they could not shake off their expectation of honourable dealing from unscrupulous antagonists. They had to deal with a system, fiscal, judicial, and administrative, which included ancient abuses in all their luxuriance; and with a people, ignorant and bigoted, whose minds are much more obedient to their religious than to their political superiors. The state of these religious superiors, the Catholic hierarchy and clergy, is indeed enviable: their large properties are exempt from taxation, by a continuance of the old privilege of the middle ages, while their persons are subject only to the jurisdiction of their own order. If a priest stands charged with grave crime, such as infanticide, or highway robbery, he is taken before the episcopal authority, and detained for examination: by some unaccountable negligence, he presently escapes, nor has any example been known of a priest being actually punished. Their education, and indeed the whole education of the Valais, such as it is, is and has long been under the superintendence of the Jesuits.

The wonder seems rather to have been, how a

good and liberal Government ever became established in the Valais at all: perhaps this might never have come to pass, if the excitement of the Lower Valais prior to the revolution of 1840 had not been permitted at least, if not favoured, by the clergy in that region. And while the disadvantages of the position were thus serious, even the men who had stood most ardent and forward in that excitement did not afterwards act in such a manner as to lend effective support to the Government which they had themselves contributed to set up. The most pronounced among them formed the society called Young Switzerland; who, while they found themselves unavoidably in collision with the privileges of the clergy, and amidst a controversy carried on with great exasperation on both sides, took no account of the difficulties of the Government, but were harsh in their reproaches because more was not done, and thus weakened a weak Government still further. The clergy defended the maintenance of their privileges by the most emphatic enforcements and denunciations of the pulpit: and their mode of warring with the political society called Young Switzerland

F

deserves particular mention. The Bishop of Sion issued a mandate forbidding the clegy to administer the sacraments to any member of Young Switzerland, or to any of their relatives, or to any reader of their journal called *The Echo of the Alps*: it should be added, that the clergy had at the same time a journal of their own, called *The Simplon Gazette*, which employed in their cause the most vehement partisanship. The scandals which arose out of this excommunication were monstrous, and furnish a further example of the abuse of religious agencies for political purposes by the clergy of various Cantons of Switzerland. Furthermore, in order to defeat constitutionally those measures which were especially odious to them, the clergy made efficient use of their influence over the popular *referendum* : thus among other laws, one for ameliorating the wretched system of public education, and another for distributing military charges with an equality which did not respect clerical immunities, were rejected by the people after having passed the legislature.

Under these circumstances, the Lower Valais became more and more the scene of lawlessness and conflict between individuals of different political parties. On the other hand, the Upper Valais partook less in this discord: its inhabitants were more unanimous among themselves, unfriendly to the Liberal Government from the beginning, and still more unfriendly to it in consequence of the continued opposition of the clergy. In 1843, the election in the Canton returned a small majority hostile to the Liberals; and an Executive Council was constituted with a majority of the same sentiments, yet not strong enough to take any decisive part. It was under these circumstances that the leaders of the Upper Valais, with the connivance of the Executive or at least of some of its members, carried on for months together a secret and illegal military organisation of the inhabitants; marched to Sion in May 1844; were enabled by the treachery of the Executive to forestal and break the preparations of the disunited Bas-Valaisans; became masters of the Government, proclaimed the latter to be rebels, and then, being joined by their own partisans in the Lower Valais, vanquished them in various encounters, especially on the river Trient. In this defeat—with its consequence, the complete extinction of the Liberal party in Valais —there was more bloodshed, more cruelty, and more brutality, than had ever before been seen in the civil dissensions of Switzerland. And to crown the whole, the Bishop of Sion issued an order to his clergy forbidding them to administer the sacraments of the Church to the dying combatants of the Liberal party. When we consider that these combatants were Catholics, as well as fellow-citizens, on the point of death, and when we reflect besides on the consequences which the Catholic Church connects with the absence of the sacraments at such a moment, it is difficult even to imagine the feelings under which so monstrous a mandate was issued.

The Government of the Valais, after the elections of 1843—if we are to call it by that name—at least the majority of the Executive Council, appears throughout this transaction in the character of a conspirator: privy to the illegal organisation of the Upper Valais—secretly conniving at it until it was completed—issuing proclamations against these Upper Valaisans, when known to be on their actual march to Sion—directing them to disband as an unauthorised and illegal armament keeping at a distance, by perfidious assurances, the Lower Valaisan volunteers under M. Barman, who had armed, though unprepared, after and on the news of the actual march of the Upper Valaisans, and who might have got into Sion first, if they had not relied upon such false assurances of the Government—inviting the Upper Valaisans into Sion, then immediately converting them from an illegal body of Corps Francs into authorised troops of the state, and making use of them to crush the Lower Valaisans under M. Barman, these latter being then proclaimed as the only rebels, and delivered into the hands of men more properly rebels than themselves. To play such a part, was bad enough in the Government of the Valais; but it was the climax of disgrace that the presiding Canton Lucerne consented to play the part along with them. It appears that the illegal organisation of the Upper Valais, known from the beginning to a portion of the Executive Council of the Valais, was still better known to the leaders in Lucerne, and concerted with them beforehand; M. Bernard Meyer, the Lucerne Secretary, making private visits to the Canton during the previous months as an underhand auxiliary. On the 13th May, 1844, when the Upper Valaisan volunteers were actually on their march to Sion, M. Meyer appeared in the latter town, carrying a commission of Federal envoy in his pocket, to be produced or not according as it might suit his views: if the Lower Valaisans under M. Barman had been victorious, he would have shown himself as commissioner, and would have employed the Federal authority to arrest their progress; but so long as the Upper Valaisans were in full advance, he was a partisan, attending the private meetings destined to facilitate their entry into Sion. As soon as they had entered that town and received the recognition of the Government, M. Meyer lent his best aid not only to the maintenance of the new Government, but also to the denunciation of the opposite party as rebels. His conduct was from the beginning that of an unscrupulous party-man, infringing the most sacred obligations incumbent on a Federal superior, and unredeemed even by any sentiment either of candour or of mercy towards the vanquished: for his language, even at the subsequent Diet, towards the Barmans and their fellow exiles, who were in this case less of rebels than the victors, was harsh and fierce in the extreme. Lucerne received its reward by the passing of the Canton of Valais into the hands of the Ultramontane or clerical party, and by its adjunction to the League of Sarnen.

It may be proper to mention—though nothing of importance turns upon it in reference to the preceding narrative—that the Executive of the Valais had, on the 4th May, on the ground of the lawless state of the country, sent a secret message to Lucerne invoking Federal intervention. This proceeding first became known in the Valais itself through the newspapers of Lucerne; and strong reproaches were addressed to the Government for having done so; upon which the Government disavowed having made such an application. They produced what they affirmed to be the copy of their letter sent, which differed from the letter received at Lucerne; there was some fraud or mystery about this letter, which was not fully explained. However the fact may stand as to the letter of request, the presiding Canton, on receiving it, issued a requisition for a Federal army: which, partly from unavoidable delays, partly from mistrust in some of the Cantons invited to furnish it, was not in a situation to enter the Valais until after the complete victory of the Upper Valaisans.

The excitement which these events caused throughout Switzerland was prodigious. The combats at the river Trient and other places in Valais, which had been disputed with great bravery on both sides, and severe loss to the vanquished — the harshness and cruelties exercised by the victors—more than all, the numerous body of exiles, many of them the most respectable men in the Canton, who fled with their wives and families into the neighbouring Cantons of Vaud and Geneva, to the sacrifice of their property and their prospects,—all this was more than sufficient to rouse throughout a large proportion of the country both profound sympathy and vehement indignation. Upon whom did the public mind fasten as the authors of the mischief? Upon the Jesuits, and upon the Canton of Lucerne. Upon the second with perfect truth, whatever may be thought about the first. It was at this time, and in this way, that the anti-Jesuit movement first began in Switzerland; for we shall not properly understand that movement unless we take it (to use an expression of the late Lord Eldon) " clothed in circumstances "—in connexion with its antecedents and accompaniments.

It has been already mentioned that the Jesuits had for a long time been established in the Valais, with control over the education both of clergy and people. But during the years 1842 and 1843, this order appeared in unusual activity. They perambulated the Catholic Cantons publicly and ostentatiously, as missionaries and special preachers—especially Lucerne and the Valais; never before had so many Jesuits been seen in motion. In the latter Canton, they denounced the Liberal Government as impious and hostile to religion; and such was the effect of their exhortations, that on various occasions the assembled people who heard them swore to rise in insurrection on the first summons. Such language, indeed, was nothing different from that which had been used by the Catholic Clergy generally, as well in the Valais recently, as in Soleure, Argau, and Lucerne in 1840, and by the Zurich Protestant clergy in September 1839. But these Jesuit missions were of all religious agencies the most conspicuous to the public eye: they came immediately previous to the misfortunes of 1844; they were blazoned by the Catholic journals as having produced almost miraculous effects; and opponents were on this occasion quite ready to credit the Catholic statement literally—to believe that the Jesuits had really done all the good ascribed to them, or all the harm, as it would appear from the opposite point of view. It is therefore indisputable that the Jesuits had actually been employed as instruments, in preaching down the Liberal Government of the Valais, by the native clergy and the politicians of Lucerne; and what they had really done was enough to cause persons who already profoundly hated the Order to arraign them as the master architects of the whole.

The 22nd May, 1844, saw the closing scene of the melancholy tragedy in the Valais: during the days immediately ensuing, the agitation arising from it pervaded most of Switzerland, and meetings were held in many of the Cantons to demand the convocation of an extraordinary Diet. Among the rest, the Great Council of the Canton of Argau was convoked for that purpose on the 28th of May: the purpose was, to urge the presiding Canton to summon an extraordinary Diet in reference to the recent events, and to instruct the Argovian Deputies as to their votes and proceeding. It was in this assembly that the name of the Jesuits was first publicly denounced. Augustin Keller—a distinguished Catholic, and the Director of the Catholic Seminary in Argau, the same person who three years before had proposed the suppression of the Argovian convents—moved that the Deputy of the Canton should be instructed to demand from the Diet measures for the expulsion of the Jesuits from Switzerland; that order being (he urged) the great cause of the deplorable dissensions reigning throughout the country, and especially of the recent calamities in the Valais.

In enforcing this point, he dwelt particularly on the Jesuit missions which a few months before had made so much noise in the Valais; whilst he enlarged on the corrupt morals, slavish politics, and intrigues against civil authority as well as against religious liberty, which marked the history of the order. The motion of M. Keller was carried in the Council of Argau by a large majority: the Argovian Deputy was instructed to make the proposition in the Diet for expelling the Jesuits; and a circular was sent (according to custom) to the other Cantons, to request that each would instruct its Deputy in reference to the proposition.

Though the circular thus sent round for discussion among the Cantons met with no favour at that time in the various Great Councils, it was enthusiastically welcomed among the Liberal Swiss public without, and had of course presented itself to many of them as well as to M. Keller. It precisely harmonized with the existing state of their minds, overflowing with sympathy for the suffering Valaisans, and with indignation for the treacherous means whereby the late counter-revolution had been consummated: it presented to them an old enemy as the author of a new mischief—an enemy who certainly had sown some tares among the wheat, and was not wanting in will to have sown the whole field—an enemy, moreover, against whom some definite resolution admitted of being taken. It was in this temper that the proposition was received at various meetings, especially at the periodical meeting of Swiss rifle-shooters from all parts of the Confederation, which took place on the 30th June, 1844, at Basle. These shooting-meetings are in many respects the parallel of the ancient Greek festival games: they serve the same purposes of keeping alive the national sympathies and supplying the defects of a very loose political union. Abundance of speeches on the political topics of the day are usually delivered by various orators at these meetings, which are largely frequented by the more ardent Liberal politicians from all the Cantons. The calamities of the Valaisan Liberals—expulsion of the Jesuits—indignation against Lucerne as an accomplice in these calamities—were among the prominent matters which agitated the feelings of this numerous and excitable assembly. The successful Upper Valaisans hardly appeared, and their flag could not be kept up among those of the other Cantons; while the defeated exiles, Messrs. Barman, were greeted with the warmest sympathy, and subscriptions were raised for the general body of Valaisan sufferers.

If the indignation against Lucerne and M. Meyer was vehement at the time of this shooting-meeting, it became greatly heightened when the Diet was assembled, and when the question of the Valais was discussed, on the 13th July, 1844. M. Bernard Meyer on that occasion occupied the chair of the Diet; and, replying to various criminations from the Deputies of other Cantons, he not only avowed, but actually boasted of, the share ascribed to him in the counter-revolution of Valais. He admitted the deliberate conspiracy and long-concerted military organisation in the Upper Valais to effect a counter-revolution, together with his own previous knowledge as well as concern in it; he justified all the previous measures by what he called the happy termination of everything; and his fierce language against the Liberals of the Bas-Valais, at that time prostrate and in exile, would have been hardly tolerable even had their antecedent conduct been that of the most guilty rebels. His speech excited indignant comments from the Deputies of Vaud, Thurgau, and

Soleure, and contributed much to swell the previous animosity against Lucerne. On the voting of the Diet, no majority was obtained, either to approve or to disapprove the conduct of Lucerne: the approvers were only the seven states constituting the League of Sarnen, together with Appenzell Inner-Rhoden; while the majority declared against all further interference of the Diet in the affairs of Valais.

The proposition of Argau for expelling the Jesuits from Switzerland was brought before the Diet; but it obtained no votes except those of Argau and Bale-Campagne—one vote and a half. None of the Great Councils in the other Cantons instructed their Deputies to support it, though it had become more and more popular among the Liberal public without. And in this state probably the question would have rested, if the Jesuits themselves had remained as they then stood—established merely in Valais, Friburg, and Schwytz. But in the months immediately following, the important step was taken of introducing them also into the presiding Canton Lucerne, and that too under circumstances in themselves eminently aggravating. The two streams of feeling, each arising out of the catastrophe in the Valais, but both at first separate — the feeling against the Jesuits, and that against Lucerne—became in this manner confluent, each tending to exaggerate the other. Their united force broke down all the obligations of intercantonal morality, and led to the flagrant political wrong committed by the Corps Francs in invading Lucerne; at which point we shall arrive in the next letter.

LETTER V.

Oct. 2, 1847.

I RECOUNTED in my last letter how the Anti-Jesuit feeling in Switzerland first arose, as a direct consequence of the catastrophe in the Valais; how it rapidly got hold of the mind of the Liberal public; and how the expulsion of the Order was first submitted to the Diet in July 1844, on the proposition of Argau, but obtained no votes except those of Argau and Bale-Campagne. That same catastrophe had also provoked a vehement animosity against the presiding Canton, Lucerne, as a treacherous accomplice in the counter-revolution of the Valais for the profit of Ultramontane politics and of the Sarnen League.

It was at this period, and under this state of Swiss feeling, that the Canton of Lucerne, hitherto unconnected with the Jesuits, and before 1840 decidedly adverse to them, determined for the first time to introduce them, and to confide to them the care of its Cantonal education. The leading men in the Canton knew perfectly well the storm which it would excite among the larger half of the Confederacy, as well as the resistance which it would call forth from a large minority of their own Cantonal citizens: lastly, they knew how much it would offend the expressed feelings, and even endanger the stability, of those Cantonal Governments which had declined to support the proposition of Argau in the Diet. Of this latter fact, the preceding debates in the Great Council, and the instructions given to their Deputies in the Diet, had presented sufficient warning. The Great Council of Zurich had passed the following resolution:—" The Deputy of Zurich is instructed in the name of his Canton to intimate the conviction that the Order of Jesuits contributes by its doctrines as well as by its missions to embitter the mutual relation between the Protestant and Catholic confessions in Switzerland; and that it thus exercises a disturbing influence on the political harmony of the nation. The Canton of Zurich therefore expresses its regret that some Cantons have received this Order among them; and intimates its wish, in the spirit of confederate brotherhood (den freundeidgenössischen wunsch), that these Cantons may withdraw from the influence of the Jesuits, and that their fellow Catholic Cantons may of their own accord resist the farther extension of the Order." This was the voice of a Great Council then in majority Conservative, and of a Government in which the Conservative Dr. Blüntschli was the leading member: it was rendered, moreover, yet more significant by the antecedent circumstances. Ten thousand citizens of Zurich (the total population of the Canton being about 230,000 souls) had signed a petition to the Great Council, praying that the vote of the Canton might be given in favour of the peremptory motion of Argau at the Diet: it was known that these signatures had been collected in a short time, and that the sentiment which they represented was much more widely spread. The Government of Zurich resisted this petition, but resisted at much disadvantage; for they could not take the ground (nor were they disposed to take it) that the admission of Jesuits into any one Canton, especially into a presiding Canton, was a matter in which the rest had no concern—they admitted that it involved both mischief and danger to the whole Confederation. "If you grant thus much," argued the supporters of the petition, "does not the spirit of the Pact, and the general obligation of ensuring internal tranquillity which it expressly imposes on the Diet, require the expulsion of the Jesuits, though the letter may be silent?" Dr. Blüntschli and his colleagues were here unfavourably placed: against a strong popular feeling supported by considerable plausibility of reason, they had to maintain the danger of going beyond a strict construction of the Pact, except where extreme necessity might compel an appeal to its spirit; and to maintain this principle—of cardinal importance, yet appealing only to a far-sighted reason—against exciting allusions to the great Protestant name of Zwingli, of which they had themselves made so much use in rousing the people to arms in September 1839. It was evident that the resistance was ruining their hold upon the Cantonal population; and in point of fact, the elections of the next year put an end to their majority. Under such circumstances, the friendly wish, addressed to the Diet and to Lucerne by a Conservative Cantonal

Government, came with double emphasis, conveying full warning of the consequences if it were not wholly or partially complied with. That wish was addressed not merely by Zurich, but by the many other Cantonal Governments who thought the Jesuits a public mischief to the Confederacy, without deeming themselves authorised by the Pact to support a vote of expulsion. Now, under such circumstances, one may indeed assign sufficient reason why those Cantons who already had Jesuits, and who, moreover, were not presiding Cantons —Friburg, Valais, and Schwytz—might decline to comply with the request for dismissing them; but it is not easy to imagine how the Canton of Lucerne, not already having them, could bring itself to introduce them immediately afterwards for the first time—in direct contempt of the antipathy manifested by a large portion of the Confederacy, and of the "friendly wish" of another large portion, expressed without the insulting appearance of coercion. We must take this fact into consideration when we look at the extraordinary excitement which follows: immediately after the people have put forth their deep and widespread conviction that the existence of Jesuits even in non-presiding Cantons is mischievous to the entire Confederacy, the very next following incident in Swiss history is, that the Order, besides maintaining itself in Friburg, Valais, and Schwytz, makes the conquest of the presiding Canton also.

It has been often attempted to bar all such considerations by simply saying—" This is a case wherein the Federal Pact imposes no restriction, and gives to no other Canton a right of intervention: Lucerne chooses to exercise its right of sovereignty, and there is an end of the matter." So the question might be argued, indeed, simply and nakedly, if there were a Federal Court about to give judgment on it; but in the conduct of life, the right of others to step in and hinder is only one portion of a wider argument, and cannot be discussed apart. There are a thousand things which you ought not to do, though other persons may have no right to hinder you from doing them: and if this be true of a private man, still more is it true of a statesman—most of all will it hold good for the presiding Canton of a dissentient and imperfectly cemented confederacy. As presiding Canton, you are under serious obligations to the entire Confederacy: you are made aware that a large fraction of it construes the Pact so as to dispute your right altogether; and that another large fraction, admitting your right because they determine to adhere to the strict letter of the Pact, nevertheless pronounce the exercise of it to be mischievous, and conjure you to abstain. Surely this is a case in which it will not suffice simply to assert and reassert that you have an incontestable Federal right: the exercise of the right must further be shown to be essential to some paramount individual interest or individual duty. How far Lucerne took any pains to show this, may be judged by the language of M. Siegwart-Müller, then President of the Diet in that town. " The Radicals and Protestants," said he, " have poured out their venom on the Jesuits everywhere: so much the more necessary is it for those Governments who love order to introduce the Jesuits." Here the extreme, though unmerited odium, attached to the name of the Jesuits throughout a large portion of the Confederacy was admitted, and converted into a positive reason for introducing them into Lucerne. What wonder that the harmony of Switzerland has perished, when the directing Canton adopts such maxims for its rule of proceeding?

Shortly after the Diet, the question of inviting the Jesuits into Lucerne, and confiding to them the Cantonal education, was brought into formal discussion before the Cantonal Great Council. The missions of the Order during the preceding year had been made to work strongly on the public mind; and the majority of the Cantonal Education Council had also pronounced in favour of introducing Jesuit superintendence — not without a strong protest from the minority, and vehement marks of repugnance from a considerable part of the population, especially in the town of Lucerne. The discussion in the Great Council was long and turbulent; but the proposition for admitting the Jesuits was carried in the affirmative, by a large majority, on the 24th October, 1844. It was subsequently submitted to the general body of the citizens throughout the Canton, for the exercise of their veto. Though nearly all the citizens in the town of Lucerne voted against it, a majority throughout the rural districts declared in its favour, and it became confirmed law.

During the discussion of the measure in the Great Council, the opposing minority urged as one of their many grounds of objection, that it violated one of the articles of the constitution, and therefore could not be entertained as an ordinary project of law, but only under the forms and conditions prescribed for revisions of the constitution. This objection was overruled by the majority; but it was nevertheless made the ground of a formal protest, drawn up, signed, and published, by five of the leading members of the minority, including among them Dr. Casimir Pfyffer, one of the ablest jurists in Switzerland. It represented moreover the full belief and conviction of the Liberal minority throughout the Canton, and aggravated their discontent arising out of genuine hatred to the Jesuits. So strongly did this discontent manifest itself, at the moment when the law was accepted by the majority of voting citizens, that the Government was induced to arrest and imprison many of the most forward Anti-Jesuits in the town of Lucerne.

It was at this point, the beginning of December 1844, that the aggressions of the Corps Francs commenced.

I have already described the different feelings which had been roused in the Liberal and Radical population of Switzerland by the catastrophe in the Valais: indignation against Lucerne, for treachery in discharge of the presidential duties—indignation against the Jesuits, whose missions had been employed as instruments to bring about the counter-revolution in Valais—and both now materially heightened during the preceding three months, by the conduct of the Lucerne Government in adopting the Jesuits, precisely at a time when the majority of the Cantons expressed their friendly wish that the Order might be dismissed even from those Cantons where it previously existed; one of the actual reasons for such adoption being (as Mr. Siegwart-Müller proclaimed in the Diet), that the Jesuits were unjustly hated in many parts of Switzerland. To these feelings was now added a new cause of excitement—sympathy for the minority in Lucerne; who believed, and made others believe, that their Cantonal constitution had been violated for the purpose of introducing the Jesuits, and who were suffering arrest and imprisonment for their resistance in a cause eminently popular. All these feelings conspiring, created in the Liberal and Radical public throughout Switzerland an animosity against the Lucerne Government, so violent that they lost all sense of political right and wrong, and resolved to put it down by the most unwarrantable employment of force.

The first Corps Francs who invaded Lucerne were not numerous, and were apparently altogether unorganised: the invaders had been apprised of the number of malcontents in the town of Lucerne, and expected that an insurrection would have broken out there as soon as they were heard to have crossed the border; but no insurrection took place. The Government easily repelled the invaders, and proceeded to very severe steps against the malcontents, real and presumed, in the town. Many of them were arrested and imprisoned; while those who escaped, or fled to avoid such treatment, were yet more numerous. During the winter of 1844–45, there were not less than 1100 exiles from Lucerne spread through the neighbouring Cantons: and this contributed to aggravate still farther the pre-existing animosity against the Government of Lucerne. It is to be remarked, that in none of the various revolutions which Switzerland has experienced, has there ever been harsh treatment of a mulitude of individuals, or any numerous body of exiles spread through the neighbouring Cantons, except in the two cases of Valais in May 1844 and Lucerne in the beginning of 1845. These are the only two cases of political disturbance or revolution in which there has been any severe reaction, visited upon a number of individuals within the Canton and driving a still larger number out of it: and both of them produced an extraordinary effect in exciting the violent sympathies of the neighbouring Cantons.

In consequence of the first invasion of the Canton of Lucerne by citizens from other Cantons, on the 8th December, 1844, an extraordinary Diet was summoned at Zurich (which had become presiding Canton on the 1st January, 1845), at the beginning of the following year. This Diet continued in session for two months, until the third week in March. Resolutions were adopted, strongly condemning the Corps Francs or volunteers violating by arms the territory of other Cantons, and requiring each separate Canton to incorporate in its legislation prohibition and punishment of such persons. But the excitement in the Cantons surrounding Lucerne was too great to be restrained by any such efforts; and some of the Cantonal Governments had no sincere desire to restrain it. On the 30th of March, a second invasion of the Canton of Lucerne was organised, in conjunction with the exiles: this time the invaders were numerous, not unprovided with artillery: and the plan of attack was concerted deliberately beforehand by Colonel Ochsenbein and other considerable persons who accompanied and took command of it. These invaders or Corps Francs were formed of volunteers from the four neighbouring Cantons of Berne, Soleure, Bale-Campagne, and Argau; the Governments of which all connived at the proceedings. Colonel Ochsenbein with his division and cannon actually reached the suburb of Lucerne, though not until nightfall: it is alleged that had he immediately commenced an attack, or fired a few shots, the Government would have abandoned the town; but the account published by the Government itself does not countenance such a supposition. Lucerne was not unprepared for the attack, and had organised an alliance with Uri, Zug, and Unterwalden, for the purpose of defence: the arrival of contingents from these allies on the following day enabled it to defeat and expel the invaders, many of whom were slain by the Cantonal Landsturm in their flight, while several hundred others remained as prisoners.

These two invasions of Lucerne by the Corps Francs are so well known, and so unanimously judged, as to dispense with the necessity both of comment and detail. If I take pains to gather together the antecedent circumstances which caused the aggressive feeling of the invaders, it is with no view of justifying such a proceeding. It was a flagrant and unquestionable public wrong, meriting all the censure which has been since bestowed upon it; disgracing the country in the eyes of Europe, and exposing the Swiss to hear from foreign ambassadors lectures the more galling because they admitted of no fair reply. Its main effect has been to weaken and hamper the party who committed it, and to fortify the position, as well as to efface in part the previous faults, of Lucerne. The preceding circumstances do not at all divest this invasion of its culpability; but they are essential to explain it—to explain that violent animosity, under the influence of which so many citizens of regular life and easy circumstances (the Landsturm of Lucerne obtained from their prisoners among the Corps Francs an abundant plunder, and in particular a large number of gold watches) were induced to imperil their lives and expend their money, besides throwing aside the most obvious restraints of intercantonal duty. The citizens of Argau and Soleure, who took arms to assist the Lucerne minority, recollected that the Catholic agitators of Lucerne had helped *their* minorities to raise simultaneous insurrections, to the infinite danger of both Governments, in the beginning of 1841; while the Cantonal Governments of Berne, Soleure, Argau, and Bale-Campagne, who connived at the organisation and march of the Corps Francs against Lucerne, had before them the precedent of Lucerne itself a few months before, when that Canton had been in privity and deliberate connivance with the conspirators who produced the counter-revolution in Valais—and that, too, in abuse not merely of Cantonal obligations, but of yet more sacred duties as directing Canton. Lastly, when it is indignantly remarked that Colonel Ochsenbein, commander of the Corps Francs in their invasion, is now in the exalted position of Chief Magistrate of Berne and President of the Diet, we must remember that he sees on his immediate left hand, as Deputy of Lucerne, M. Bernard Meyer, the director and instrument of Lucerne treachery in the conspiracy of the Valais.

If it were important to take a comparative estimate of the wrongs on both sides, we might remark that those committed by Lucerne spring from a cause at once permanent and fatal to the tranquillity of the Confederacy — the spirit of Catholic Ultramontanism and aggrandizement; while those of the Corps Francs had their rise in a state of excitement, which, however culpable, depended on a peculiar combination of recent events, and was in its nature essentially transitory. But in truth, such a comparison would answer little purpose: the important circumstance to remark is, that both wrongs are real, and that the later of the two may be traced back by a visible thread of causality to the earlier. At the present moment, both parties in Switzerland have the conviction that their opponents have acted wrongly towards them: in each, that conviction is well founded. "Convicia et probra invicem rixantes ingerunt: neuter falso." Herein lies one of the great difficulties of finding any solution for the existing complication of affairs.

I have touched upon the two expeditions of the Corps Francs together, because both grew out of one and the same state of excited feeling. But between the dates of the two (8th December, 1844, and 1st April, 1845), events of material importance took place—the discussion on the subject at the Diet, and the revolution in the Canton of Vaud.

At the previous Diet, in July 1844, only one Canton and one Half-Canton had voted for the expulsion of the Jesuits from Switzerland: in the Diet of 1845, ten Cantons and two Half-Cantons voted for the same proposition: so great was the difference made by the fact of Lucerne, the presidential Canton, having adopted them in the interval. Zurich, presiding at the extraordinary Diet convoked in January 1845, did not support the proposition for expelling the Jesuits, nor recognise the competency of the Diet to do so: but its circular address proclaimed in the strongest manner the mischief, insecurity, and discord, which the reception of the Order into the Catholic directing Canton would be sure to excite in Switzerland, and urgently invited Lucerne to revoke its resolution. It is to be remarked that the Jesuits had not yet actually come into the latter Canton, though the law had been passed to introduce them. The Zurich circular farther insisted that the character of the Order was not to be considered as purely religious, but as partly political, partly sectarian and controversial: its direct aim being to aggrandize the Church at the expense of the State, and the Catholic religion at the expense of the Protestant. From the first of these two tendencies, it is repugnant to a large portion even of the Catholic world; from the second, it is placed in hostility with the Protestants; and both reasons concurred to render its admission into the presiding Canton of Switzerland disastrous, as a direct aggravation of the two great sources of discord inherent in the Confederacy. The language of the Deputy of Geneva, then strongly Conservative, on the subject of the Jesuits, was of the same tenour; though he voted against the resolution for expelling them, on the ground of want of competence in the Diet. There needs no farther argument to shew that the Anti-Jesuit feeling in Switzerland was a perfectly genuine and substantive feeling—not a mere pretence got up for the purpose of revolutionizing the Pact, as so many persons have argued. Here were Deputies expressing the same Anti-Jesuit feeling as strongly as it could be expressed, who yet would not support a sentence of the Diet for expulsion. Indeed, the whole past history of the Jesuits, from the commencement of their Order, betokens an organised and systematic teaching of religion, not for religious ends, but as a means for procuring political and social ascendency: other priests have done the same to a greater or less extent, but none except the Order of Jesus has become notorious as reducing it to rule, craft, and professional duty. It was against this tendency, not against any matters essential to the Catholic religion, that even the Catholic world protested in the last century, when the Order was abolished: it is against the same tendency that the opponents of the Order protest at present; though they doubtless greatly exaggerate its present power to do mischief. The argument has often been urged—"What prodigious harm can seven Jesuits in Lucerne (the number at first introduced) effect, to justify such strong excitement?" But it is to be recollected, that when the Great Council of Lucerne first determined to adopt the Jesuits, no one knew to what extent they would be employed. There was every reason to believe that they would be made actively available in prosecution of those Ultramontane intrigues which Lucerne had been pushing, both as Canton and as Vorort: they had been so turned to account in the Valais, and their agency might be indefinitely extended: moreover, it is to be remarked that the name *Jesuit* cannot be heard, on the Continent, without a cluster of odious associations derived from the past—and that the proclamation, "The Jesuits are coming!" is really more terrific than the men so called when they stand before you in flesh and blood. The Corps Francs invaded Lucerne before the Jesuits were actually in it: they did not invade Friburg, where the Jesuits had been long established. It was the double and confluent sentiment, against the Jesuits and against Lucerne, which roused them to the pitch of armed aggression.

It was on the 14th of February, 1845, during the sitting of the Diet, that the revolution of Vaud occurred. Vaud is the Canton immediately adjoining to Valais: its citizens were almost witnesses of the battles in the preceding May in that Canton, though without taking the least part in them: its surgeons and its *ambulances* went across the border to administer succour to the wounded on both sides: it received and fostered the greater part of the exiled sufferers; the two chiefs of whom, Maurice Barman and Colonel Joris, escaped into its territory only by swimming the Rhone, after having exhausted every effort of brave commanders. From all these circumstances, the excitement in

Vaud, arising out of the Valaisan catastrophe, was unusually great; and the two feelings in which that excitement manifested itself—animosity against the Jesuits, and animosity against Lucerne—became proportionably aggravated. The Deputy of Vaud, though the Government of the Canton was then what is called Conservative, and did not support the vote for expelling the Jesuits in July 1844, expressed the strongest indignation when M. Meyer of Lucerne avowed in that assembly his long cognizance of the conspiracy for counter-revolutionizing the Valais. If such was the strong feeling general in Vaud in July 1844, much stronger did it become during the months immediately succeeding, when Lucerne, in defiance of the sentiment expressed throughout the larger portion of Switzerland, passed the law for admitting the Jesuits; and when the Lucerne minority, through the consequences of their opposition to that measure, were cast into banishment and spread through the sympathising Cantons. When the Great Council of Vaud met for the purpose of instructing their Deputy in prospect of the Diet convoked for the last week in January, a petition was presented praying that he might be directed to support in the Diet two points—expulsion of the Jesuits from Switzerland, and amnesty for the Lucerne exiles. This petition, signed by no fewer than 32,000 persons, was supported by a minority both in the Executive and in the Legislative Council; but the majority of both were opposed to it.

It was asserted by some of those who opposed this petition—what has been so often asserted of petitions emanating from Swiss Radicals—that those who signed it did not really care about the substantive thing asked for, but only asked it as a means to arrive underhand at the abolition of the Cantonal sovereignty and the erection of an Unitary Government in Switzerland. A similar insinuation had been made in the preceding month of July in the Great Council of Zurich, by Dr. Blüntschli, in reference to the 10,000 petitioners of that Canton, who asked for the expulsion of the Jesuits: it was a remark captious and unseasonable, overleaping causes obvious and forcible in order to arrive at others which were at once weaker and more distant; and it was likely moreover to irritate petitioners who knew themselves to be in earnest. How widely the feeling displayed in the petition was diffused throughout Vaud, is proved by the number of signatures: for the total population of the Canton is only 190,000 souls, and 32,000 signatures must represent seven-eighths of the qualified voters under a system of universal suffrage. According to political maxims very widely diffused in Switzerland, it was contended by the supporters of the prayer of the petition, among other reasons for granting it, that this enormous majority ought of itself to be imperative, and to overrule any objection which the Council might entertain. In England, no such general maxim would be admitted: but we may safely assert, that if ever the time should come when five millions of petitioners (about the same proportion of our population) demand anything at the hands of Parliament, and are known to care for it intensely and earnestly, that petition will not be refused, even though it contain matter more questionable than the two items demanded by the 32,000 persons who signed in Vaud. The majority of the two Councils in the Canton of Vaud, refused to comply with the prayer of the petitioners. To wait for the return of the quinquennial elections, and then choose a Council of different sentiments (which would have been the constitutional course), while in the mean time the Cantonal vote would have been given in Diet to sustain the Jesuits and the Government of Lucerne—appeared intolerable to a population all excited on one and the same immediate point. We may doubt whether even the English people would have submitted thus to wait if they had been baulked at the moment of their feverish excitement about the Reform Bill in 1832 : and it is to be noted, that no Swiss constitution contains any provision analogous to the power of discretionary dissolution of Parliament by the English Crown. The immediate result of the refusal of the Councils was, that large numbers of armed citizens from the neighbourhood, marched into Lausanne ; while the Government, on calling out the militia, found that this force was disposed to act not against, but in unison with, the insurgents. The movement throughout the Canton appears to have been not less unanimous than passionate : the Councils were forced to abdicate, and a Provisional Government was formed, at the head of which was M. Druey, the leader of Opposition. It is right to mention, that in this revolution no man sustained the least damage either in person or property. A new constitution, more popular than the preceding, was drawn up, and accepted by the people during the ensuing summer: but in truth, the preceding constitution had also been very popular, and was so regarded even by Radical writers who wrote during the year 1844: so that the new constitution worked no violent transfer of the seat of power, and was more analogous to a change of Ministry in England, with a dissolution of Parliament, than to the ideas commonly suggested by a revolution.

The proceedings of the former Government of Vaud, by which they had in part lost popularity before this change, would be instructive to remark upon, inasmuch as they illustrate the subsequent conduct of the pastors and the reaction against the latter which manifested itself under the new Government. But upon these I do not touch, since they have no direct bearing on the Federal politics, to which the present letters are chiefly confined.

LETTER VI.
Oct. 9, 1847.

THE perilous disposition to unauthorised employment of force, which had pervaded Switzerland during the winter of 1845, was quenched by the repulse of the Corps Francs from Lucerne on the 1st of April, disastrous and humiliating to the last degree. The Governments which had connived at it were under the ignominious necessity of negotiating with Lucerne for the ransom of their prisoners; which they obtained at the cost of between 500,000 and 600,000 francs: besides which sum, Lucerne claimed and received from the Diet, assembled in July, a further indemnity of 150,000 francs for damage sustained, out of the general Federal treasury. Resolutions strongly condemnatory of Corps Francs were again passed at that Diet; and it must be added that from the 1st April, 1845, to the present day, the peace of Switzerland, as between Canton and Canton, has never once been disturbed: every one of the

Governments has manifested an unshaken determination to maintain it, and to repress individual "sympathisers," if they attempted to march in armed bands across their own Cantonal border.

But though the spirit of armed invasion had thus been extinguished, the political feeling continued unaltered; and the elections of 1845 in the Canton of Zurich returned a majority in the Great Council which displaced the Government called Conservative, the offspring of the 6th September, 1839. That Government had maintained, as long and as much as it could, a sympathy with the Lucerne politics, which at length robbed it of its popularity with the citizens of the Canton, though none of the latter had taken part in the expedition of the Corps Francs. In the Diet of July, 1845, the expulsion of the Jesuits from Switzerland was again discussed: ten Cantons and two Half-Cantons voted for it; nine Cantons, including Geneva, against it. St. Gallen did not vote at all; its Great Council were equally divided on the question, 75 for it and 75 against it,

To the question of the Jesuits, the one great matter of controversy during 1845, was added in the early part of 1846 the formation of the armed separate league called Sonderbund, between Lucerne, Uri, Schwytz, Unterwalden, Friburg, Zug, and Valais. Formal announcement of this league with its conditions was made to all the Swiss Governments: in point of fact, these same seven Cantons had long before been connected by a league called the League of Sarnen; but their new organisation, called the Sonderbund, brought with it the important addition, that it became professedly an armed confederation—its members bound themselves to furnish contingents of men and money, and to obey a common military authority —all announced to be exclusively for purposes of common defence. To this is to be added the still more important fact, that the Cantons of the Sonderbund not only bound themselves by covenant to arm, but actually did arm and organise themselves, providing means of offence as well as means of defence. The question was thus raised, Is a separate league, thus armed and organised, contrary to the Pact, the sixth Article of which says expressly—" No alliances shall be formed by the Cantons among each other, prejudicial either to the general Confederacy or to the rights of other Cantons"?

This question was brought before the Diet at Zurich, for the first time, on the 4th September, 1846, by the proposition of the Canton of Thurgau to declare the Sonderbund illegal. Ten Cantons and two Half-Cantons voted in favour of this proposition,—Berne, Zurich, Glaris, Soleure, Schaffhausen, Argau, Tessin, Vaud, Thurgau, Grisons, Appenzell-Exterieur, Bale-Campagne. The seven Cantons of the Sonderbund voted against it, together with Appenzell-Interieur. Neufchatel, St. Gallen, Geneva and Bale-Ville, did not vote at all, but referred for fuller instructions to their Cantons. Neither on this question, nor on that of the expulsion of the Jesuits, which was again discussed, was any majority of the Diet obtained.

So these two questions stood over, to be re-discussed in the Diet of the present year. But the year 1846, and the first half of 1847, produced events in Switzerland which materially altered the second discussion as compared with the first. Revolutions took place in Berne and Geneva; a revision of the constitution in Bale-Ville; and the attainment of an electoral majority in the Great Council of St. Gallen.

The revolution of Berne, properly speaking, was only partially connected with Federal politics, and would not have been much spoken of in connexion with them, if it had not happened to raise to the Presidency so marked a man as Colonel Ochsenbein, the previous commander of the Corps Francs. For in truth, the Government of M. Neuhaus, which Colonel Ochsenbein supplanted, was just as much Radical and Anti-Jesuit, and would have been, if it had lasted, just as much against the Sonderbund, as himself: and it is one among many proofs of the loose use of names as applied to Swiss political parties, that M. Neuhaus is spoken of in 1845 as the leader of all the Radicals, and in 1846, though his politics had not at all altered, as a Conservative, merely because he stood opposed to Colonel Ochsenbein. After the repulse of the Corps Francs from Lucerne on the 1st April, 1845, the Government of M. Neuhaus, which had before connived at them, thought it necessary to make demonstrations against them, and to take some steps calculated to prevent any repetition of the attempt. In this they were certainly right, whatever censure they may deserve for their previous connivance: moreover, it may be remarked, that in the state of widespread excitement which preceded the 1st of April, their interference would probably have been of little effect, had they really applied themselves to the task; whereas, in that state of depression which succeeded the repulse, there remained only a provoked minority anxious for farther action, and that minority was not too large for the Government to control. The anger and vexation which pervaded a large mass of the people after the defeat of the Corps Francs was pretty sure to vent itself upon some one; and the Government of M. Neuhaus, disavowing and beginning to repress what it was known to have previously connived at, became the object of discontent with a considerable party which took Colonel Ochsenbein for its leader.

The opposition against the Government of M. Neuhaus thus doubtless began in causes connected with Federal politics; but it was enabled to succeed by agencies of a totally different character. It collected together all the financial malcontents and embarrassed interests from the different parts of the Canton, promising some special Government intervention to meet the particular case of each. The proprietors of land in the communes of the Bernese Oberland were distressed and surcharged with mortgages at high interest: to them was promised an advance of 5,000,000 francs from the funds of the Government at an interest of 5 per cent., 1½ of which was to be laid by as a sinking-fund for repayment of the principal. This was to be ultimately enlarged into a general *caisse hypothécaire* for the whole Canton. Next, the communes of the Emmenthal were borne down by the weight of pauperism: to them was offered an enactment relieving each separate commune from legal liability to maintain its own poor, and making that charge public or Cantonal—at the same time consolidating the poor-funds of all the separate communes into one aggregate Cantonal poor-fund, whereby the richer communes would have borne a large part of the charges of the less affluent.

Such was the scheme as originally projected, though not carried into full effect: its tendencies appeared so dangerous that it met with the most strenuous opposition in passing through the constituent assembly, and was ultimately modified so as to leave to every commune its own poor-fund apart, but at the same time to alter for the future the principle of poor-law relief from compulsory to spontaneous, and to abolish the legal claim of a poor person on his commune. This latter change is recognised in principle, and is to be gradually approached in practice: over and above the amount of the poor-fund (which of course remains consecrated to its original purpose), the amount of compulsory rates hitherto levied upon the different communes is to be gradually diminished, until at length, after the lapse of four years, no farther recourse is to be had except to voluntary collection. To smooth this transition, and to aid the distressed communes, the Cantonal treasury is to furnish to each commune assistance proportioned to the amount of its rates: but the aggregate charge thus arising on the Cantonal treasury is not to exceed in any case the maximum of 400,000 Swiss francs (about 600,000 French francs, or 24,000*l.* sterling: the population of the Canton is at present about 430,000 souls). It will be seen, that in the poor-law thus modified, the change first projected, or Cantonal aid to the pauperised communes, was retained in principle, but much contracted in extent; while the new provision of abolishing compulsory poor-rates was introduced.

Lastly, a third financial operation, besides what related to mortgages and pauperism, was included in this same party move. The communes of the Seeland and other parts of the Canton were subject to various burdens of immemorial antiquity— tithes, rent-charges, &c., old feudal redevances attaching to the different districts, and which had passed into the hands of the Cantonal Government when it first conquered or purchased the seigneurial rights, and under which of course the land had often changed proprietors. These burdens had always been odious, from their association with the ideas and feelings of feudal superiority; after 1798, the Helvetic Republic then framed had tried partly to abolish, partly to commute them: but this was found impracticable, and they were ultimately rendered redeemable at a rate which the Government of M. Neuhaus in 1845 had reduced from eighteen to twelve years' purchase.

His opponents promised a still further reduction to six years' purchase; and inasmuch as by such a step those who had already redeemed at the higher rate would be placed in a worse condition, an indemnity was insured to them out of the public treasury, equal to the difference between the higher and the lower rate. This operation has since been carried into effect; and its result has been, that the Government has had to pay out in the way of indemnity (partly to private impropriators of tithe, partly to those who had before redeemed at the higher rate), a greater positive amount than all which it received of principal money from redemption on the reduced scale. It thus not only ceases to receive for the future a certain tithe-revenue, but has incurred a positive loss.

The defalcation arising in the public revenue out of these various operations, is to be made up by imposing a direct property-tax upon the entire Canton, excepting only those Catholic portions which formerly constituted the Bishopric of Basle, and which are subject already to an *impôt foncier* of fixed amount. The property-tax—a painful novelty to the Bernese—has been distinctly announced in perspective, but not yet actually levied: it is to be hoped that the actual collection of it, which is now become indispensable to cover a large deficiency in the public revenue, will not prove too unpopular to be carried into effect.

Such were the various financial combinations whereby the party of M. Ochsenbein gathered together sufficient support to displace M. Neuhaus, procure a constituent assembly, and frame a new constitution. In that constitution the new financial changes stand embodied, though in point of fact they have no proper right of admission into an act of political constitution: they are all serious matters of legislation, proper to be considered and settled by the elective Councils which that constitution may provide: they threaten, moreover, to embarrass greatly the future state of the revenue. The new constitution, politically speaking, is an improvement, since it substitutes direct election of the Great Council in place of election by two stages: but this would hardly have been sufficient of itself to displace the former Government, which might well have adopted such a change if recommended by popular feeling. Considered with reference to Federal politics, the revolution of Berne in 1846 is of no great moment: considered with reference to internal affairs, to the stability of public property, and to the precedent afforded of acquiring partisans by helping embarrassed debtors out of the public purse, it is one of the most unpromising which as yet occurred in Switzerland. It was accomplished merely by popular meetings and demonstrations, without the use of arms on either side: M. Neuhaus was displaced during the winter, the Constituent Assembly held its sittings through the spring, and the constitution was published and ratified by the popular vote in July 1846.

On all these points the Revolution which occurred at Geneva on the 7th of October, 1846, was materially different. It was of great Federal importance: it was purely political, a triumph of Radicals over Conservatives, without any appeal to pecuniary interests: moreover, it involved a serious armed contest. The proximate cause of it was, the debate and decision in the Great Council respecting instructions to be given to the deputation at the Diet in reference to the Sonderbund and the Jesuits. I have already mentioned, that when the former question was discussed at the Diet on the 4th September, 1846, the Deputy of Geneva reserved his vote; and in the beginning of October, the Executive Council of Geneva proposed to the Great Council a draft of instructions for his future conduct.

After 1814, the year of liberation from France, the government of Geneva became representative in principle, yet with a restricted suffrage and little responsibility to the people. Though confined to the hands of the old Genevese families in the Upper Town, however, it was administered with liberality and intelligence, and formed in this respect an honourable contrast to the retrograde and reactionary spirit which animated nearly all the Swiss Governments between 1815 and 1830. Hence, the vehement burst of popular feeling which traversed Switzerland after 1830, remained for a long time without much effect on Geneva; nor was it until 1841 that a movement at length broke out which that Government was unable to resist: a new constitution was then framed, with suffrage substantially universal, and with the voters distributed into ten electoral colleges. The practical working of this system was, to transfer the real power from the Upper Town to a combination of the Upper and Lower Town, and to throw the Radicals of St. Gervais into a minority. The politics of Geneva have been not a little influenced by its topography: the Rhone divides the town into two unequal parts— the larger part on the left bank containing the Haute and Basse Ville, while the smaller part on the right bank forms the district called St. Gervais. The Haute Ville or Upper Town contains the Hotel de Ville, the public buildings, and the residences of the old families or aristocracy of Geneva —men wealthy and prudent as a class, socially as well as politically exclusive, and proud in the recollections of the ancient town when it figured during the seventeenth and eighteenth centuries as a refuge for persecuted Protestantism, and when its professors and clergy, enjoying European celebrity, added some dignity to a government essentially narrow and repulsive. The Basse Ville contains the bourgeois of various occupations, merchants, tradesmen, &c., who are separated from the aristocracy of the Haute Ville by a social line not the less felt and observed because it is nowhere traced on the map. On the opposite side of the river, in St. Gervais, dwell the artisans and operatives, with smaller tradesmen among them: a class industrious and energetic, as well as intelligent—of independent spirit—strongly attached to theories of Democracy and social equality, and hating priestly dominion not less than political privileges—moreover, though last not least, every man among them more or less a soldier, possessing his rifle and familiar with the use of it. The movement of 1841 had been one in which the Basse Ville joined with St. Gervais to abrogate the privileges of the Haute Ville: but when the new constitution was formed and put in working, the result of it was found to be that the Haute and Basse Ville combined together against St. Gervais—aristocracy and bourgeois against the Radicals. The newly-allied parties seem to have acted under a persuasion that universal suffrage was in itself dangerous and full of bad tendencies which it was their duty to neutralize; and for this purpose they constituted themselves a government of resistance. Their principal supporters formed themselves into secret societies, both in the Great Council and out of it, which were made to act powerfully upon the elections as well as upon legislative proceedings: and so strongly did the tide of party organisation set among these Conservatives, that whoever among their own number declined to join some one of these societies, was looked upon coldly and unfavourably. The effect of such organisation was of course sensibly felt, and the existence of the societies as a general fact well known by the Radical leaders. M. James Fazy in the Great Council, and others, commented upon them severely under the usual title of " les embrigadés." To the Radicals, moreover, the symptoms of aristocratical pretension in the newly admitted members of Government from the Basse Ville—who had united with them to bring about the movement of 1841, and who but for that movement would not have been accounted worthy to occupy the chairs of the Executive Council—were more galling than those same dispositions would have proved in the members of the old families whom they had been so long accustomed to see in the seats of power. The Genevese Government between 1841 and 1846 was thus in its political spirit a government of resistance as well as of party; though its administration then, as well as before 1841, gave little ground for complaint. It commanded a large majority in the Great Council; but it had the considerable and compact minority of Radicals in St. Gervais in strong opposition—on one occasion, indeed, in 1843, in actual revolt, which was only put down by force. M. James Fazy was the leading Radical representative in the Great Council.

Upon this state of dissentient parties fell the passionate course of Swiss Federal politics during the interval between 1841 and 1846. The Radicals of Geneva sympathised strongly with the feeling against the Jesuits, and still more strongly with that against the Sonderbund in 1846. On the first of these questions, the Government of Geneva, while refusing to concur in any vote for expelling the Jesuits out of other Cantons, as a matter beyond their competence, always expressed their strong opinion that the Jesuits were noxious to the peace of the country, and invited other Cantons to dismiss them voluntarily. This reserve did not suit the views of the Radicals; nevertheless, on the question of the Jesuits, the Government obtained large majorities and an easy triumph. With the question of the Sonderbund their course might have been even easier, since there was really less difference of opinion: but it was rendered unnecessarily difficult, and became ultimately even critical and perilous, from the political feelings with which the Government approached it in October 1846, in proposing the instructions for their Deputies at the future Diet. There were two points to be determined: first, whether the Sonderbund should be declared illegal; next, what security should be provided against renewal of the Corps Francs, which the Cantons of the Sonderbund set forth as one of their main justifications for the formation of the separate league. Now on neither of these points does there seem to have been any substantial difference of *opinion* between the Government and the Radicals—both agreed that the Sonderbund was contrary to the Pact, and both agreed that the Corps Francs ought to be repressed. But though there was little difference of opinion, there was an immense difference of *feeling* between the two parties: the Government did not approve the Sonderbund, but it cordially detested the Corps Francs and the vein of feeling in which they had originated; while the Radicals on their part did not approve the Corps Francs, and were nowise unwilling to concur in prohibiting them, but their positive hatred was directed against the Sonderbund and its originating sentiment. Now the Government, even though consenting to declare the Sonderbund illegal, were most afraid of appearing to give a triumph to Radical principles: accordingly, they proposed to instruct the Deputy, while pronouncing the illegality of the League, to couple his vote with such strict conditions respecting the Corps Francs as would probably not have been realized, so that he would have been prevented from forming one of a majority against the Sonderbund. Moreover, M. Demole, the first Syndic of Geneva, one of the most vehement Anti-Radical speakers in Switzerland, would probably have gone to the Diet with these instructions, and would have given all the right of the case, and all the weight of the Cantonal authority, to the Lucerne side of politics, even while pronouncing that Canton to have gone further than the Pact justified, in forming the Sonderbund. The instructions thus proposed by the Government, repugnant in the extreme to the Radical minority, were Anti-Radical to so impolitic a degree as even to offend many of their own partisans in Council; several of whom supported an amendment, moved by one of their number (M. Senn), which was a certain approximation towards the Radical view, and as such was supported also by M. Fazy and his friends, though rejected by the Government. Ultimately the original instructions were carried, but by a majority much smaller than the Government were in the habit of obtaining. Moreover, there were other points in these instructions which provoked the displeasure of the Radicals, such as the proposition made to appoint Federal Representatives in restraint upon the recently formed Radical Government of Berne, when that Canton should become Vorort on the 1st of January, 1847. Such a power is given to the Cantons in the Pact, but has never yet been actually exercised; and the mere proposition of it was a party move indicating a dislike of Radicalism, which the Radicals on their side were not backward in repaying.

As soon as the instructions had passed the Council, vehement manifestations of discontent broke out in St. Gervais: meetings were held; and M. Fazy with others proclaimed an indignant protest, to be addressed to the Vorort, against the resolution taken by the Council. This was regarded as a decided act of illegality by the Government, who thought it their duty to arrest M. Fazy. He refused to obey; and the Radicals of St. Gervais, full of sympathy for him as well as indignation against the course of political affairs, rose in insurrection to defend him : while the Government, trying to overpower them by military force and by cannonade, found itself worsted in the attempt and obliged to abdicate. For all ordinary purposes it was doubtless strong enough, but not for such an act of force as the arrest of the popular leader under the existing state of feeling. No one, however, seems to have been prepared, certainly not M. Fazy himself, for the spontaneous burst as well as the obstinate determination manifested by the Radicals. When once political dispute passes from words to arms, new forces which before slumbered are found to awake, while those which were before in evidence fall short of their apparent promise, in a way which renders calculation of the result extremely difficult, and throws much to the score of accident.

The strong and unmixed political character of this revolution—the courage manifested by the men of St. Gervais—and the absence of reactionary lawlessness after success—rendered it a most impressive event throughout Switzerland; and its future influence upon Swiss affairs will be the greater, inasmuch as it has elevated M. Fazy, known before only as an able Opposition speaker and journalist, to a post wherein he has been enabled to display powers of positive government and organisation for which few had given him credit. In the constitution as now changed, the elective franchise remains nearly the same in extent, having been before practically universal;

but it has been distributed anew; the aggregate of about 12,000 voters is now divided into three electoral colleges, instead of ten, while the number of members in the Great Council has been diminished by one half. On both these points the previous arrangement was highly favourable to the influence of the Genevese aristocracy, who have thus by the present change lost an underhand advantage adroitly infused into universal suffrage by the constitution of 1841. In all times of political quiet, a wealthy aristocracy like that of Geneva will be able to sway more or less the fair expression of electoral opinion, even under the present or any other system: but they cannot reasonably expect that the constitution should be so framed as to help them in the work. The most questionable change introduced by the new constitution appears to be the election of the Executive Council by the aggregate body of Cantonal electors, instead of by the Great Council, as is the practice in the other Swiss Cantons. But we may remark, in regard to the Genevese constitution of 1847, what was already observed about the new constitution of 1845 in the canton of Vaud—that it does not bring about any capital transfer of the seat of power : it is a change from universal suffrage, partially hampered and laid open to corrupt influence, to universal suffrage more free and spontaneous. But the 12,000 electors continue now, as before 1846, to constitute the political sovereign ; and the large majority now possessed by the Radicals in the Great Council is probably more owing to the strong temporary stimulus of the revolution itself, than to any inherent difference between the working of the present and the former systems of election. Whether that large majority will be durable, depends much on the conduct of the Radical Government; but under all circumstances it may well be considered doubtful.

Bale-Ville has always been inflexibly Conservative down to the beginning of the present year, in sympathy with Lucerne and its allied Cantons. The rich mercantile aristocracy of Basle forms in many respects a parallel to that of Geneva, and the minds of its population were strongly affected by the revolution in the latter. At the beginning of the year 1847, political discontent being on the increase in Basle, the Government were prudent enough to take warning by the occurrences in Geneva, and to determine on a revision of their constitution, which is supposed to have averted the chance of a revolution. Since that revision, the Federal politics of Bale-Ville have assumed a neutral or a juste-milieu character; neither supporting the Sonderbund nor voting with the majority.

The vote of St. Gallen, at the Diet of the present year, was determined by the elections of last May for the Great Council of the Canton. Previous to last May, the Great Council was divided into two parties equal in number, so that at the Diet of 1846, the Canton gave no vote on the questions of the Jesuits or the Sonderbund. In May last, the elections for the Catholic district of Gasters returned new men, of the Liberal or Radical party; and this gave a majority, though a small majority, to that party in the Great Council. St. Gallen is a Canton of parity, divided between Catholics and Protestants, with equal political rights to each confession: the population is about three-fifths Catholic and two-fifths Protestant, not inhabiting continuous districts, but Catholic and Protestant communes intermingled one with another. There exists moreover in this Canton what is called the Confessional Separation,—a distinct organisation of both confessions, apart from and to a great degree independent of the Government, for the management of all that relates to religion, education, matrimony, and a range of other matters connected with these general heads. There is a Catholic Council of Administration, elected by the general body of Catholics, and a Catholic Executive Board, chosen by that Council: and as the fund belonging to the confession is ample, this board is well paid, exercises great influence, and is almost a match for the Government itself. Moreover, a Bishop for the Canton exclusively has recently been named, and endowed, together with several Canons, out of a remaining portion of the property belonging to the old Abbots of St. Gallen. The Catholic religious leaders in that Canton have thus received a reinforcement which will make their organisation even more effective than it has hitherto been in correspondence with

Lucerne, and may probably enable them to break down the present narrow majority. The knowledge of this fact is of course familiar to the Government of Lucerne; who have even been led to doubt whether the Great Council of St. Gallen, with so small a majority, would go so far as to sanction measures of execution against the Sonderbund: this explains in part the language of inflexible determination and defiance which they have maintained.

The two votes of Geneva and St. Gallen, added to the ten and two half-votes of 1846, constitute the majority against the Sonderbund and the Jesuits in the Diet of the present year. Bale-Ville, which was before favourable to the League, is now in a position of neutrality.

I have now followed down the course of Swiss Federal politics from their causes in the past to their present condition. One letter more—containing some general remarks on these past facts, and on the probable tendencies of the future, in so far as they admit of being dimly discerned—will close the series.

Letter VII.

Oct. 16, 1847.

We trace a distinct though complicated sequence of events, one growing out of another, from the politico-religious movements prior to 1840 down to the present Diet and its votes respecting the Sonderbund. It is impossible even to comprehend, still less fairly to appreciate, the feelings and position of Switzerland at present, without going back to these previous circumstances. If the Sonderbund is to be characterised as an effect resulting from the expeditions of the Corps Francs, these expeditions resulted even more directly from the peculiar train of events which preceded them in 1843 and 1844. And it has been the more necessary to go briefly over these, because the actual condition of Switzerland is usually presented in a totally erroneous point of view—as resulting from the systematic efforts of the party called Radical to merge the Cantonal sovereignty in a unitary government, and to oppress the Catholic religion.

The invasions of the Corps Francs—the real wrong for which the Radicals of four Cantons adjacent to Lucerne are responsible—had their rise in neither of these dispositions. It seems, indeed, strange that the Radicals should be so often charged with preference for a unitary government, since Radicalism, as such, could not possibly gain, and would in all probability lose, by the change; for it is certain that government has less weight as a substantive force apart from the people, and that the demagogic influences are more perpetually operative, in the separate Cantons, than they would be in the case of one concentrated system pervading all Switzerland. If any one reads M. Tillier's valuable History of the Helvetic Republic down to the Act of Mediation in 1803—a time during which the comparative fitness of the unitary and Cantonal systems of government was really under serious deliberation, which it never has been since —he will see that one of the objections urged by opponents of the Cantonal system was, that it opened so many easy and tempting markets for demagogic speculation. Some particular Radical leaders might gain in importance by a unitary government; but the greater number of them would be personally losers—to say nothing of the feeling common to the population of every Canton, which puts all idea of unitary government out of the question. Nor is the alleged hostility towards the Catholic religion on the part of Radicals at all better founded. Hostility to the Jesuits is not hostility to the Catholic religion: still less was the act of suppressing the Argovian convents a proof of this latter feeling; for the real persons who have gained by that suppression are the Catholic ministers, Catholic schoolmasters, and Catholic parishioners of the Canton; while the means of inculcating the Catholic faith and duties are unquestionably strengthened and not weakened. The monks of Muri did not employ their property for any such purpose; though they were ready enough to assist politico-religious agitation, either in their own Canton or in others.

The series of facts set forth in the preceding letters, sufficiently shews that the two parties in the Federal quarrel are not distinguished from each other by systematic respect or disrespect for Cantonal independence. On the two matters of contention which have stood out most prominent—the suppression of the Argovian convents and the maintenance of the Jesuits—the position of the two parties in respect to Cantonal rights has been reversed. On the first of the two, the Radicals were the upholders of Cantonal sovereignty, which was then held very cheap by Lucerne and its allies; while on the second, Lucerne has pushed its separate rights to their extreme limits (as may be seen from the language addressed to that Canton by the Conservative Cantonal Governments, nowise unfriendly to Lucerne), against the Anti-Jesuit feeling enforcing a wide construction of the Pact. If Lucerne in 1842–43 had been able to obtain a majority in the Diet for the unconditional restitution of the Argovian convents, and had Argau refused to obey, the Cantons now forming the Sonderbund would have marched out their entire military force to execute it, at any cost of bloodshed: they would have left to Radicals all the talk about sanctity of Cantonal rights. It suits their policy now to take stand upon unrestrained Cantonal omnipotence; but when we put 1843 and 1847 together, we may see plainly that this forms no fixed line of distinction between the two parties.

That which runs through the Federal quarrels during the last seven or eight years is, not so much the disputed competence of Canton against Diet, as the struggle for ascendency between the Catholic church and the political power. The success of the Catholic priestly agitators in the revision of the Lucerne constitution in 1840— their attempt, even by force, to accomplish a similar change in Soleure and Argau—the subsequent events connected with the Argovian convents, the Valais, and the Jesuits—all these are under one form or another the continuation of the struggle above mentioned, brought into prominent relief by the action of Lucerne both as Canton and as Vorort. That Canton has put itself at the head of the Catholic *Clerocracy* (if we may venture to add one to this already numerous family of compound words) of Switzerland, working through Democratical forms, and adopting the Jesuits as the most effective of all trainers for a political priesthood; while on the other hand the party called Radical, including both Catholics and Protestants, throughout Switzerland, have been brought together by common antipathy to this movement—of which antipathy the great and perfectly natural manifestation has been, the protest against the introduction of Jesuits into Lucerne. We here discover the real pivot of Swiss Federal dissensions during the last few years; dissensions which have divided the country into two hostile camps, and have given to the proceedings of the Diet a positive and central character foreign to its habitual negation and impotence. Of course each Canton has had its own local parties and grounds of dissension, and with these the Federal politics have blended, often in predominant proportion. In Zurich, in Vaud, and in Geneva, the then existing Conservative Governments were placed in a false position,—anti-Jesuit in theory and pro-Jesuit in vote,—which distinctly caused the overthrow of the two former, and mainly aided in that of the latter. Allowing for such separate Cantonal individualities, it is not the less true that the general cast of Swiss parties is as follows.

1. The *Clerocracy* of Lucerne, working for the

promotion of Catholic priestly ascendency throughout Switzerland—ultra Democratical in constitutional forms, and leaning upon the veto or *referendum* as a means of nullifying the lay representative council. 2. The Radicals of both confessions—bound together chiefly, if not entirely, by a strong common antipathy to what may be termed the Lucerne policy. 3. The Conservatives, principally Protestants, distinct from both—adverse to the Radicals (who form their own immediate opponents), and thrown by this circumstance into sympathy with Lucerne, which does not always proceed from coincidence of views—now generally in opposition, except in Neufchatel and partially in Bale-Ville, having been elsewhere elbowed out by the stronger contentions between the two other parties. The conduct of Lucerne has indeed been such as to do much unintentional service to the Radicals its opponents, and much mischief to the Conservatives its supporters.

Such is the manner in which the contending parties now stand opposed in Switzerland: the main antithesis is that between lay-power and priest-power, each working through Democratical forms — the same line of parties, substantially, as that which now divides Belgium; whilst the powerful organisation of the Catholic Church, pervading as it does so large a portion of the country, and applied as it has been systematically to convert political questions into religious, is in truth a much stronger restraint on Cantonal sovereignty than the feeble powers exercised by the Diet. The purely political question, between privilege on the one side and the sovereignty of the people on the other, is one of subordinate moment in Switzerland. The former creed is not found convenient to proclaim anywhere as a party formula, even by those who regret the times anterior to 1830: either the Landsgemeinde, or universal suffrage with or without direct expression of the popular voice in veto or *referendum*, prevails everywhere; and the competition lies between the priest and the magistrate, which of the two shall influence that voice, or in what proportions it shall be divided between them. Throughout the Cantons of the Sonderbund, and amidst much of the Catholic population in the other Cantons, the larger share of such influence is in the hands of the priest: in the Protestant Cantons, the sphere of the latter is much more limited, in spite of a frequent disposition to extend it by direct political preaching. The difference between popular government under Catholic priestly ascendency and under lay ascendency, is strikingly manifested in the fact, that in the Cantons of the Sonderbund there is at this moment no free expression of opinion on the part of the minority: not only is the Cantonal press under restraint, but even Liberal newspapers, published in other Cantons, are systematically refused admittance; while in the Radical Cantons, the Opposition press is as outspoken as in any part of Europe, and every one who chooses to denounce the Government or uphold the Sonderbund is at liberty to do so.

The preceding observations on the general cast of Swiss parties are not calculated to lighten our conception of the political dilemma in which that country is now placed. On the contrary, they bring to view forcibly the points of repugnance between one part of the Confederation and another, and the difficulty of maintaining that degree of harmony which is absolutely essential to the idea of a common "Vaterland," recognised in words in the Federal Pact. The two hostile camps into which the country is now divided, and the tone of discussion hence arising, go to deprive this impressive German word not only of all hold upon the feelings but of all import and reality in argument.

If we assent to the claims and to the reasoning set up on behalf of the Sonderbund, we should be driven to pronounce the Pact entirely at an end—we should be driven to affirm that the majority of the Confederation have no right in any case whatever to bind the minority. The right of the Diet to condemn that League cannot be denied, except upon arguments which go to deny it in all and every case. It would be clear, even upon general reasoning simply, that the most essential purposes of the Pact would be frustrated if armed leagues among the separate Cantons were allowed to subsist. But this is a matter not left to inference; for the sixth Article of the Pact (already alluded to) expressly says—"No alliance prejudicial either to the general Confederacy or to the rights of other Cantons shall be formed by separate Cantons among themselves." Commentators on the Pact, such as Professor Stettler of Berne (not a Radical writer), distinctly read this clause as constituting the Sonderbund Anti-Federal; and it is hardly possible to construe it otherwise. The Sonderbund do indeed contend—" Our League is necessary for self-defence; it is formed exclusively for purposes of defence, and is therefore not prejudicial either to the Confederacy or to any other Canton: of this *we* ourselves, as sovereign Cantons, are the only competent judges, and we deny the competence of the majority of the Diet to determine it for us." Here the point at issue is distinctly raised, " Have the majority of the Diet competence to determine whether a particular league formed comes under the general description of league forbidden by the Pact?" In other words, " Have they the right to apply the general provisions of the Pact to a particular case? Or has every separate Canton a right to determine this for itself?" To concede this latter point, would be to extinguish altogether the practical obligation of the Pact. Commentators upon the Pact always reason upon it as an instrument according to which each Canton has voluntarily renounced a certain definite portion of its independent sovereignty, and in which the majority of the Diet have a right judicially to construe its provisions and apply them to particular cases, but no right to enlarge or modify them; such judicial decision being binding on the minority. Unless we grant this, the whole business of voting at the Diet, and of distinguishing between Cantons of half vote and Cantons of whole vote, would be an absurdity: indeed, the Sonderbund themselves grant it, in cases where they are the parties complaining and not the parties to be bound. Not to mention the efforts of Lucerne to procure a majority for the purpose of enforcing restitution of the Argovian convents—efforts which of course imply that the majority had a right to overrule the step taken by Argau, and to dictate an authoritative construction of the Pact—during the past session of the Diet, and at the very time when the Sonderbund formally refused to obey its resolution, the Deputy of Friburg preferred complaints to it against the

Government of Vaud, for having laid undue taxes upon the properties in that Canton belonging to the Abbey of St. Bernard. The case was one much less clear, in respect to contravention of the Pact, than the very existence of the Sonderbund itself: but whether clear or not, the Deputy of Vaud would have had a ready answer, if he in his turn had denied the competence of the majority to construe the Pact judicially, and had claimed for his Canton the right of separate and independent interpretation.

To deny the right of judicial construction in the majority when it goes against you, and to invoke it when it makes in your favour, is an inconsistency not at all likely to be tolerated. And the more we look at the resistance of the Sonderbund to the Diet, combined with the arguments whereby it is defended, the more we shall be satisfied that it amounts to nothing less than a suspension of the Pact in practice as well as in theory. If a French or an Austrian army were at this moment to cross the frontier, it is certain that they would meet with no unanimous resistance, even if they were not hailed as positive allies, by the Cantons of the

Sonderbund. The continuance of that separate armed League is plainly incompatible with the continuance of the Pact as something real, vital, and operative. Lucerne cannot be Vorort of the Confederation, and at the same time chief of a Catholic Sonderbund.

How the majority of the Diet will deal with this grave and critical conjuncture—how they will construe their Federal rights, and what degree of firmness combined with moderation they will show in exercising them—we shall see when they re-assemble on the 18th of this month. If we were to judge by the recent manifestations on both sides, we should conclude that the melancholy contingency of a civil war was all but inevitable. Berne, Zurich, and Vaud, the three most populous Cantons in the Confederation, have placed themselves in a complete state of military readiness; while the Landsgemeinden in Schwytz, Uri, and Zug, have also passed the strongest resolution of resisting force by force; and arms have been transmitted to the Sonderbund both by France and Austria. It will be seen after the 18th—first, whether all the Cantons of the majority concur in sanctioning measures of forcible execution,* in case pacific tentatives fail; next, whether the population of all or most of those Cantons heartily espouses the cause; thirdly, what species of compromise they are disposed to offer or accept, as a means of avoiding war. On none of these points can we safely venture to indulge predictions at present. If the Cantons of the majority, with their population, are all unanimous, and most of them really earnest in the cause, there can be no reasonable doubt (looking at the question merely as one of military superiority) that they could take Lucerne and Friburg, in the latter of which there is already a discontented and compressed minority: the principal force and agency of the Sonderbund resides in these two Cantons. But this alone will be very far from accomplishing what is really desired—the renovation of a Pact which has been practically set aside, and of an extinct confederate brotherhood. The population of the recusant Cantons, instead of being conciliated, would probably be still farther alienated: no man supposes

---

* All the Cantons *have* now concurred: the decision of St. Gallen having recently become known. (Oct. 24.)

that they could be permanently constrained by force, or hindered from renouncing the Confederation, should such be their confirmed wish; and in such case the separation would only become formal and avowed, without any maintenance of the Pact even in name. Mere superiority of force, assuming it to be ever so complete, lands us only in this untoward result.

We may, however, spare ourselves the trouble of speculating at present on a subject so melancholy as well as so perplexing; for a civil war would be sure to throw up contingencies such as no man can foresee—not to mention the chance of foreign intervention which opens the door to a host of new mischiefs.

The present majority of the Cantons has on its hands a grave and responsible task. They are now in a state of positive and intimate co-operation altogether unusual in Switzerland, which it is deeply to be wished that they may have the wisdom to preserve, resisting that spirit of Cantonal egoism which has hitherto constituted the chronic malady of the country. They possess by far the larger portion of the wealth, the intelligence, the industry, and the population, of Switzerland: all the progressive elements in the country, and all its means of future permanent union, reside with them. The Sonderbund may break up the Confederation, but cannot possibly guide or hold it together: all its tendencies are those of discord and disintegration—setting Cantonal individuality against Confederate brotherhood, Protestant against Catholic, one half of the Catholic world against the other half, priest against layman, and the dictation of religious preaching against the liberty of political discussion. That M. Guizot or Prince Metternich, who have every interest in the disunion of Switzerland, should patronize the Sonderbund, is extremely intelligible: that this sentiment should also be shared by those who desire to see Swiss nationality maintained, at least at such a pitch of efficiency as will defend the integrity of the territory, is more extraordinary, and has its source probably in an undistinguishing aversion to Radicalism. Even if, by some fortunate compromise, the present quarrel were appeased, it would still be an indispensable condition of future unity that the Government of

Lucerne should desist from its Ultramontane and aggressive policy, and from acting as the champion of the political aggrandizement of the Catholic Church throughout Switzerland: if such policy were renewed, the same antipathies and excitement would again be roused throughout the Confederacy.

It deserves to be remarked, that the Diet at its last meeting passed a peremptory resolution against the Sonderbund, but only a modified resolution against the Jesuits—*inviting* each Canton to dismiss them, but not putting forth the language of command. This, in point of fact, is no more than what has been expressed as a wish even by the Conservatives. We may perhaps infer from such difference of language that the majority of the Diet is not likely to be unanimous in insisting upon the worst part of its case—the expulsion of the Jesuits from Schwytz, Friburg, and Valais. If this shall be publicly declared, it will be a material step towards narrowing the ground of contention, and depriving the Sonderbund of its common motive for resistance. And it seems not wholly impossible that the present excellent Pope might think the motive of restoring peace in Switzerland sufficient to warrant his interference, and might enjoin the Jesuits to withdraw from Lucerne. In the present excited state of the country, however, with the party manœuvres of an active Opposition in each separate Canton, and with the taunts thrown out against the majority that they are afraid to execute their own resolutions—no man can reckon on the dispositions necessary to a moderate compromise on both sides: not to mention the chance of some accidental collision on the borders of Friburg or Lucerne, which might produce a state of ungovernable exasperation, and destroy all chance of adjustment.

There is so much of all that constitutes both the good man and the good citizen distributed throughout Switzerland, that the present dissensions which agitate that country cannot but inspire a profound and anxious interest. Industry, forethought, self-supporting energy, and reciprocal dispositions to neighbourly help, pervade a larger portion of the population than perhaps in any other country of Europe. Of the spontaneous tendency to order which prevails there with the minimum of police agency, a striking proof is afforded by the fact that there were no food riots in any part of the country throughout the last winter and spring, though the distress was of the severest kind, the price of bread in some parts even higher than in London, and the necessity for extraordinary private aid unexampled. Of none of the neighbouring countries can the same thing be said: in France, Germany, Italy, even in England, such riots were but too notorious. Political revolutions have undoubtedly been frequent in Switzerland: but these revolutions have rarely been attended with any loss at all, either of life or property; and never in any case, except Lucerne and the Valais, have they produced any harshness, or cruelty, or multiplied exiles. Proprietary rights have never been disturbed, and are especially protected by the fact that property in land is widely disseminated among the people. In most of the Cantons, the Small or Executive Council addresses every year to the Great Council a report of its annual administration, and the series of these reports forms a record of the internal government of the Canton. If we follow that series for the larger

Cantons, such as Berne, Zurich, St. Gallen, Soleure, &c., we trace proofs of an improving and corrective administration, and the greatest pains taken to turn limited powers to the best account. In particular we observe gradual and systematic amelioration in the management of the Communes, resulting from increased activity of Cantonal superintendence: the Commune is the unit of Swiss social life, and its common funds as well as its common obligations are of the most essential importance to the comfort of the citizen; both the one and the other have been subjected to good rules, and rescued from neglect and jobbing, without at all extinguishing the principle of distinct Communal management. The two grand items of expense which figure in the budget of a Swiss Canton, are the roads and public education: the sums which have been bestowed on both these purposes since the changes of 1831 have been immense, relatively to the total means of the Cantons. The habit of borrowing money on the security of Cantonal or Communal credit, has happily obtained little footing in Switzerland: far from being disposed to spare themselves by throwing burdens on successors, the Swiss think it necessary to get together and keep together a capital which shall produce interest—a school-fund or poor-fund—so that the weight of annual taxation for the purpose may be lightened : the actual generation thus imposes burdens upon itself greater than those which will be borne by the succeeding. Elementary education is nearly universal; and in many Cantons, the public sentiment, even among the poor population, sustains the principle of making it compulsory. The dark side of the picture presents itself in increasing pauperism, as in so many other countries of Europe : the poor families multiply but too fast, and a proletary population appears to be augmenting in the manufacturing Cantons; and this is unfortunately an evil which, when once established, contains in itself a principle of contagion spreading more and more. The indirect taxes, from which a large proportion of the Cantonal revenues are derived, have tended everywhere to become more and more productive; but it seems that the difficulties by which Swiss manufactures are surrounded in respect of sale of their products, by the restrictive systems of other nations, are found almost insuperable even by present capitalists, and are at least likely to check further increase. In many of the Cantons much has been done since 1830 to improve the security and facility of the relation of lender and borrower on landed security, by means of cheap and authentic registration of mortgages and sales, and in some cases even by formal *cadastre* of the territory. It is only since 1831 that any general habit of canvassing public affairs has obtained among the people: before that period, neither the proceedings of the Great Council nor even the Cantonal budgets were in general published. This new activity of public life, and strong attachment to the theory as well as the practice of popular government, has produced its full crop of political dissension; but it has at the same time awakened a zeal for turning the powers of government to profitable public account, and a sensibility to the exposure of wrong or abuse, which have already manifested themselves in a thousand beneficial ways, and which present every chance of improvement in the future.

The Cantons of the Sonderbund are in every respect the stationary and backward portions of the Confederacy. It would be unjust and unreasonable to disturb their population in a state of things suitable to their feelings; but there will be the deepest reason for regret, if the preservation of that which they cherish is found, through the intrigues of their partisan Vorort, to break up the union, arrest the progress, or endanger the independence, of the larger and more improving Cantons. Whether such shall be the case or not, the intelligence of the next two or three months, so full of anxious anticipation, will reveal.

Supplemental Letter.

To M. ALEXIS DE TOCQUEVILLE (*Député*).

London, Dec. 21, 1847.

I AM glad to hear, by your letter received a day or two ago, that you have at last been put in possession of the third and fourth volumes of my History of Greece. They ought to have been delivered to you much earlier; my bookseller had orders to send them immediately on their being published, and the delay which occurred is to me surprising, as well as vexatious.

I have desired a few copies of my letters on Switzerland to be sent over to Galignani at Paris ; and orders will be given to Galignani to deliver your copy to you, if you will take the trouble of asking there for it. I shall be very glad if you will read them before your debates come on in the Chamber : whether you will agree in all points with the opinions which I give, I do not know ; but the value of my letters consists in the series of facts which they set forth, showing that the anti-Jesuit movement cannot be understood except in connection with the peculiar circumstances which preceded it. You will see that I sympathize with the Diet, or (as it is called by its opponents) the Radicals: which does not at all mean that I defend everything that they have done.

The manner in which the war has terminated exceeds everything which my most sanguine hopes could have anticipated. I never ventured to expect that 90,000 citizens would have turned out at the orders of the Diet, not only to brave all the perils and all the hardships of war, but also to execute with perfect order and system all the commands of an able general. I never ventured to expect that the Sonderbund would have displayed so little of that resolution, at the moment of trial, which was so much extolled before the moment arrived. Lastly, I never expected that M. Guizot and Prince Metternich, having so admirable a game to play, could have been guilty of such extravagant blunders. These three chances have all turned out so much better than any one could have reasonably predicted, that I am almost tempted to augur (my mind being now very full of Herodotus and his point of view in reference to human affairs) that there must be some countervailing misfortunes in reserve for the Diet. When I left Switzerland, I came away with very melancholy anticipations as to the prospects of the country. I fancied that the Sonderbund, aided by Guizot and Metternich, would be quite strong enough to keep Switzerland disunited and helpless, if not to tear it entirely in pieces. The magnificent and unanimous military demonstration which the people have just made has been the salvation of the country—not merely from the loss of its political existence and independent working, but also from the spread of that degrading fanaticism over the Catholics of Switzerland generally, which was the only engine for the Government of Lucerne to operate upon.

You know that I am no great admirer generally of Lord Palmerston, and that especially, in regard to his proceedings in 1840, I strenuously and publicly condemned him. But his conduct during the present year, both in Italy and in Switzerland, appears to me to have been no less prudent than liberal; while I quite agree with you in saying, that Guizot has committed, in regard to the latter, almost all the faults which a Government possibly could commit. It will be a great misfortune, if, in consequence of the strong anti-English prepossessions common to all the parties in France, he is enabled to throw the blame of his own blunders on the alleged hostility of Lord Palmerston. Guizot and Metternich were in reality the accomplices and allies of the Sonderbund, in the most barefaced manner, for the purpose of treading down and humiliating "Radicalism" in Switzerland: they constituted themselves parties in the case, and arrogated to themselves the right of interpreting and enforcing the Swiss Federal Pact: putting themselves out of condition to act as impartial mediators and arbitrators. So far from wishing to prevent war, it was they who got up the internal war, in order that they might have a pretext for interfering. What right can they have to complain of Palmerston because he would not sympathise in such a policy, or that he refused to concur in any intervention except one purely amicable, and confined to a case of pressing necessity? It will really be a pity if a few adroit sentences about the "*Machiavelism*" of Palmerston and of England, should enable Guizot to escape from the censure which his conduct so justly deserves. He has made his own position completely for himself: he has endeavoured, by a furious and calumnious use of the press, and by the aid of the Conservative press in Switzerland, to persuade the French people that the Swiss majority had neither courage nor conduct, and were unfit to manage their own affairs: he has been accusing them of intentions which are not only untrue, but are the reverse of the truth, e.g., a disposition to put down cantonal sovereignty and establish an unitary government. The truth is, that his hatred of Radicalism is so intense as to blind him to all rational estimate of what is before him: he has been the dupe of the lies of his own partisans. And the result of his manœuvres has been, that he has strengthened Switzerland at home, and the cause of Radicalism generally in Europe, more than any Swiss patriot or Radical could at all have calculated on doing.

You will perceive that my Swiss Letters do not go beyond the 18th or 19th of October, just the time when the Diet resumed its sittings after adjournment. But the events which happened after that period, and before the actual commencement of war, are important to understand: if you will procure the files of the *Constitutionnel*, which has had a very good correspondent in Switzerland, from the 18th of October to the 7th or 8th of November, you will follow the series of facts without much labour. In particular, I beg you to remark the conduct of the majority of the Diet, as well as that of the Sonderbund, in reference to compromise, immediately before the war. The Sonderbund made no offer to treat at all—no offer at all tending to procure peace—until *after* the 25th October, the day on which the Austrian Ambassador wrote to the Diet to acquaint them " that he should withdraw in case war broke out, but that his Government *would not interfere* in the war for or against either party." The next day (or next but one), after this intimation of the Austrian, the Sonderbund communicated certain terms on which they would consent to dissolve their separate league. These terms were not a diminution, but *an enlargement* of their demands :

for they required that not only the question of retaining or expelling the Jesuits, but also that of re-establishing the suppressed Argovian convents, should be submitted to the determination of the Pope. This reference to the Argovian convents was in reality the introduction of a new element of dispute, and of a demand more inadmissible than anything concerning the Jesuits: for it reopened a question which had been formally decided by the Diet in 1843, and which the Diet could not possibly consent to submit to arbitration anew, thereby reversing its own former determination. You see thus that the Sonderbund really made *no* offer of *compromise* at all—no offer to surrender a portion of the disputed ground in order to keep the rest. But the majority of the Diet, in the private conferences which took place immediately before the Sonderbund Deputies left the Diet, really did make a very genuine and serious offer of compromise. They offered to leave the Jesuits undisturbed in Friburg, Schwytz, and Valais, provided the Government of Lucerne would dismiss them from that Canton. This was peremptorily refused by the Sonderbund. You will see this stated in the Proclamation of the Diet, issued 4th November, immediately before going to war, which I beg of you to read: it is so good, that our newspaper the *Times*, in its fondness for the Sonderbund, suppressed the document.

I felt particular satisfaction—sympathising as I do with the majority of the Diet—that they had offered this compromise in order to avoid the evils of war. *At that time*, it was the reasonable and fair compromise: for the admission of the Jesuits into one of the three presiding Cantons always appeared to me to be much more open to complaint from the other Cantons, than their admission (or rather their continuance) in Friburg, &c. Now that the evils and hazards of war have *actually been incurred*, I think the Diet are quite right to turn the Jesuits out of all Switzerland: but the case stood very differently before the war, when there were chances on both sides.

To think of the blindness of Guizot and the Sonderbund, in refusing to compromise on such terms! The dismissal of the Jesuits from Lucerne alone would really have been but little loss to the Sonderbund party and little gain to the other:

the real Jesuit power was in Friburg and the Valais, and their expulsion from those Cantons is a serious blow to their influence everywhere. If the Sonderbund had accepted the compromise then offered, and consented to dissolve themselves, they would have remained hardly less strong than before the dissolution. For while the same Governments remained in the seven Cantons, the mere formal act of proclaiming that the league had ceased, would have been of very little practical effect, and pretexts might easily have been found for renewing it afterwards. Moreover, the large majority in the Diet would still have remained, breaking up all harmony of political action, and the policy might still have been pursued, with hardly less chance of success, of trying to fanaticise the minds of the Catholics all over Switzerland. The acceptance of that compromise would have been a partial defeat *in name*, for the Sonderbund, but a victory in *substance and reality*; and it would, in all probability, have sown the seeds of disunion among their antagonists, the majority—many of whom would have been much displeased at the offer. Fortunately for Switzerland, the Sonderbund refused the compromise, and took the chances of war: it was absolutely necessary for Guizot that a war *should* break out, in order that he might have a pretext for intervention.

I think you will be inclined to consider the Sonderbund party (when you read my Letters) as a knot of men trying to turn religion to political account, and to put the priest above the political leader; employing for that purpose all the artifices of an ultra democracy: unfortunately, the Conservatives of Geneva, Neufchatel, and Basle, and elsewhere, have lent their support to this party, without any direct sympathy with its objects, but from ungovernable hatred of their political rivals, the Radicals—the same monomania which now besets Guizot. There never was any mistake greater than that of supposing the Sonderbund to represent religious liberty: on the contrary, it represented an intensity of Church predominance and power, such as could not have existed anywhere but in these Cantons, and such as has now ceased to exist even in *them*. Nothing, in my judgment, can be more important than the general principle of leaving every man to that form of religious belief and practice which he approves: but when a band of men (like the Jesuits) confederate for the express purpose of making religion an instrument of political power, they become most proper subjects for interference, restraint, or expulsion (in case of need), on the part of the magistrate. I do not understand how Guizot will prove that he has promoted the credit or the permanent ascendency of France by identifying himself with these "ligueurs" of the nineteenth century, and by employing these traitors (who are now proved to have been in correspondence with, and to have borrowed money from, Austria) as means for disuniting and dismembering Switzerland. The principle which he laid down about that country appears to me to be most unjust and detestable, treating it as a country which was to be governed, not according to the choice of its own people, but according to the *bon plaisir* of the allied Powers. Believing, as I do, that his end was thoroughly mischievous, I will not quarrel with him for the egregious mistakes which he has made in the means. Intending the direct contrary, he has been really the great creator and sustainer of Swiss nationality—he has brought about the greatest and most important revolution which has happened in the country since 1798, and has imparted to the people a sentiment of force as well as of union, which Radicals might long have prayed for in vain. Vive Guizot! You are almost the only Frenchman to whom I would venture to write so frankly and copiously about Guizot: for I know well that, generally speaking, condemnation of him from an Englishman is a sure way of procuring for him support, or at least of softening opposition against him, in your Chamber. For any one who, like me, wishes for the progressive advance of liberal ideas in Europe, and desires also to see France in the van of that movement—it is melancholy to see that the foreign policy of France has receded to the same sympathy with Austria and Russia as it had before 1830, and that we might almost fancy ourselves in 1827, as far as the French Government is concerned, instead of in 1847. I trust the nation, at any rate, will not be found to have remained thus stationary.

Adieu — my dear M. de Tocqueville — I am almost ashamed at the length of this letter. Give my very best compliments and regards to Madame de Tocqueville: I was very glad to hear from Milnes that she was well. I am pretty well, and am progressing with my Greek history.

Yours most faithfully,
G. G.